MY MULE DRINKS FROM THE GANGES

MY MULE DRINKS FROM THE GANGES

A TRAVELOGUE

GABRIEL ROSENSTOCK

TRANSLATED FROM THE IRISH BY
MICHEÁL Ó HAODHA

ACADEMICA PRESS
BETHESDA - DUBLIN - PALO ALTO

Library of Congress Cataloguing-in-Publication Data

Rosenstock, Gabriel.
[Ólann mo mhiúil as an nGainséis. English]
My mule drinks from the Ganges : a travelogue / Gabriel Rosenstock ; translated from the Irish by Mícheál Ó hAodha.
p. cm. -- (Irish researcb series ; no. 64)
Includes bibliographical references.
ISBN 978-1-936320-48-6
1. Rosenstock, Gabriel--Travel. 2. Authors, Irish--20th century--Biography. 3. Irish--Foreign countries. I. Ó hAodha, Mícheál. II. Title.
PB1399.R6Z47 2012
891.6'2143--dc23
[B]

2012010038

Academica Press, LLC
Box 60728
Cambridge Station
Palo Alto, CA. 94306

Website: www.academicapress.com

to order: 650-329-0685

This book

is dedicated to the Ayurvedic herb brahmi

CONTENTS

Translator's Note	ix
We are all travellers	1
Afterword	127
Glossary	131
Bibliography	139

PREFACE

As with its European neighbours, Ireland is home to a number of festivals which celebrate the art of travel writing, the annual Lismore Festival of Travel Writing in County Waterford to take but one example.

The modern genre of travel writing as practiced by Irish writers is very different to much of what passed for travel writing in Ireland, in recent centuries. While the vast majority of Irish travelogues as written in the past two centuries were written in English, this travelogue was written (and published originally) in Irish before later being translated and re-shaped in the English language. It

It links in with a long tradition of travel writing as published in the Irish language, a tradition that was occluded with the ascendancy of the English language in both print and public life from the eighteenth century onwards. My Mule Drinks from the Ganges- reclaims one of the oldest traditions in Irish culture – the tradition of the"immrama" – and it is therefore a book that is unique and different from an Irish context. Throw into the "pot"the multicultural melangé that are references to Eastern spirituality, Buddhism, the incredibly rich tradition that is Irish language and Celtic Christianity and a myriad of literary references and influences as relating to world cultures and philosophies and you have a intoxicating"brew" that no translator worth his salt could ignore!

WE ARE ALL TRAVELLERS

We are all travellers ... We have all travelled to where we find ourselves today. We have moved and been moved in ways visible and invisible. Think of tribes and races, advancing, retreating, since the beginning of time. We have all come about from such nomadic wanderings and searches, crusades and pilgrimages, wanderings and exiles and only when we find ourselves will the long journey end.

Are we destined to wander? Is it in our blood? If so, is it because we belong to another dimension in the first place? 'Ich bin ein Gast auf Erden…', so goes the hymn, 'I'm a guest on this earth'. Stirring music by Heinrich Schütz. Stirring isn't the word. Shattering. Schütz shatters me when I listen to that psalm. Only by being shattered can we become whole again.

Stay at home and you're still a traveller whether you realize it or not. You travel in your dreams. Or you daydream. And isn't the whole world travelling constantly around the sun?

I'm 52 and heading East. To find a part of my nature that may have eluded me? Maybe so. Maybe no wonders await me, no one to whom I can say, 'Brother!' and when I get back to Ireland I'll agree with Kipling about East and West and the twain not likely to meet.

I think of the East-West Journal that I used to read once a month. Back in the days of TM and macrobiotics when East and West began to embrace one another. That journal made Kipling sound silly. It boldly declared that we needed each other, East and West, as two hemispheres of the brain, yin and yang. But what have we really learned from the East? For most of us it's a foreign culture; beneath the veneer of tourism, let us say, or apart from alternative approaches to medicine, or Eastern influences on music and food, can we really get beneath the other's skin? Do we want to? Do we need to? Or is it our own skin we admire at full-moon parties on some beach in Thailand or Goa?

Only today I glanced at the cover of National Geographic and there was this wizened little person up to his neck in monsoon floods. He had a drowning man's grip on his most precious possession—a sewing machine. My little surreal tailor. What was most remarkable about the scene was his angelic smile. Would I be smiling in such a situation? It's a matter of what you're used to. He was accustomed to monsoons and welcomed them. Those dark, rain-bearing clouds were none other than Lord Krishna himself, bringing water to a parched continent, or the goddess Kali, 'lustrously black like a large cloud and robed with nothing but the sky …'

it begins –
clouds do not know
the length of the journey

This heat would kill a camel … First stop on our long road is Dubai. Best thing it has to offer is the air conditioning. It's eight in the morning and the heat would make a camel keel over. We make our way towards the hotel, the Howard Johnson, and from there to the nearby shopping mall, quite ugly on the outside but very presentable once we're inside.

The Arab will not use his left hand except to wipe his posterior. I've often heard this. Poppycock. I've just seen a noble Arab stroking his silky black moustache with his left hand.

What's this? A shop full of bikinis and underwear and a passing procession of unflappable lady shoppers, only the whites of their eyes visible. The heat! And they are all dressed in black. If I remember my science class, black is not the best for coping with intense heat.

Lunch is a fish called the hamour. But it's difficult to enjoy it with CNN blaring on incessantly about terrorism. Such bluster—why not add it to wind power, solar power and wave power? That would be the end of war. No one can own the sun, the wind, the tide. Not yet anyway.

Lobster in the desert …. Is fánach an áit ina bhfaighfeá gliomach, as they say in Irish: you never know where you might find a lobster—or a first cousin. Leo Keane is out here working with copying machines. (My mother was an Ó Catháin/ Keane. They came down from the North during a spot of bother in the 1640s and settled in the Fields of Athenry). We're going to meet Leo later on in a pub, where else? The Irish Village. (Say no more!)

Mmm … the coffee in Dubai is nothing to write home about. Maybe the problem is with the milk. It wouldn't be camel's milk by any chance? A dhroimeann donn dílis, I hum to myself, 'O silk of the kine …'

The people of Dubai, or the Dubs as I call them, are every bit as friendly as Dubliners though some of them have a bit of a haughty look about them. Traffic moves along sedately enough but one does encounter the occasional lunatic who thinks he's part of a camel race. One rarely hears a horn blaring or any hue and cry. Road rage hasn't reached Dubai yet. Not a voice is raised, except that of the muezzin, of course. In case we had difficulty hearing him, he's calling us to prayer through a sound system. Imagine if instead of the bells of the Angelus, our priests at home called us all to prayer from lofty turrets.

We order bacon and colcannon in the Irish Village and my mountainous portion must have arrived on my plate by way of a shovel. I suppose we are the only ones consuming bacon in the United Arab Emirates—may the Prophet forgive me.

A table quiz is the big entertainment laid on for the night. The trad group Ragús were due to play next week to celebrate five years of the 'Village'. The quizmaster is a Brit. Our team is faring badly. Roy Keane, or Manchester, or some forgotten punk band (forgotten by me at least) is the answer to every second question. The questions vary each week, of course, but I'm told the answers are usually the same.

The place is full of ex-pats and the questions—as well as the mock aggression between the teams—reflect that ghostly, tentative relationship they all have with their home country, if home they have any more. Question! The least-populated country in the world? Teams huddle and confer. Afghanistan, suggests a Scottie. The Vatican, snorts an Englishman. No Papist he. Greenland? says I. The discussion becomes heated. The Vatican is a city state, not a country, insists a pundit. This battle is being fought for a crate of beer, or for a drinks voucher to be exact. But you'll only get your prize from the off license by furnishing proof that you are not a Muslim. It seems to be a bit of a nonsense since alcohol is freely available in hotels; all you need to prove is that you have a mouth.

I send a postcard home, depicting camels racing in the desert. The kids needn't worry that I'm squandering my vast fortune: gambling is strictly forbidden, even though the richest horse race in the world is staged here, in Dubai. (I have dealt with the cruelties often involved in camel racing in my novella Lacertidae with which you are undoubtedly familiar).

The underclass ... In a small corner of a local newspaper I see a photo that disturbs me, that of some poor Asian found dead. Who was he? It appears he died of natural causes but nobody knows who he is. Natural causes? How natural was his life, here among so many millionaires? Asians do all the dirty work here, Indians, Pakistanis, Filipinos. Cleaning up after us. Are we going to see a lot of this kind of thing in days and weeks and months ahead?

The mosques are truly beautiful but the rest of the architecture reminds me of East Berlin in the Communist era. Look, look how big we are, how strong! Tá Teamhair ina féar is féach an Traí mar atá… Tara is grass and look at the state of Troy …

It's not only latrine cleaners and such like that are being exploited. Work by an Indian artist whose medium is wood is on sale here for what is probably ten times the price you would pay in India. Then again, he may have been from an area that hadn't a suitable gallery for his work. The market economy.

A dhow sails through the Creek. These boats have been trading with India and Africa for aeons. We cross the Creek in a water taxi, an abra, and view the skyscrapers that have appeared, mirage-like, from what a few short years ago was bare desert.

Now the cry is not the haunting, melodious call to prayer but 'Rolex! Rolex' and other rude mantras. Fake watches, though I didn't know it at the time. Are we getting more of a taste of what's to come? Will we be able to distinguish between the genuine article and the imitation, the real and the unreal?

Eithne buys herself a scarf in the souk, the great textile market. If you are familiar with a volume of poems of mine called Syójó (of course you are, I never doubted you), you will know that I don't wear a watch. But I break a habit of a lifetime. Time, you have caught up with me, I'm yours at last. I've never had time for you up to now, as you know, viewing things sub speciae aeternitatis. Ah well, glad to report that the fake watch fell apart the following day.

Taxis come and go like water beetles. The sun has seen enough and sinks. The waters of the creek turn purple. The world darkens. Another blast of Allah hu akbar from a mosque turret—how great Thou art!

Mystic mariner … Outside the Al Abra Cafeteria, look! A young waiter is on his knees, praying. At his eye level is an advertisement hoarding for John Player Gold Leaf. The famous logo of a bearded sailor in the middle of a life belt, a mysterious image from my youth, and for all the world you'd think the pious young waiter was adoring this iconic prophet. Of course, God is everywhere.

His prayers finished, Eithne asks him what juices they serve. She picks papaya juice.

'It's far from papaya juice you were reared,' says I, sipping a coffee. It's got sugar in it, which I never use. However, in this heat I'd enjoy anything. Unpasteuerized camel's urine. (Speaking of camels, there's not one mention of a camel in The Quran. I thought I'd mention it now; mightn't get a chance later).

Eithne can't get over the kandoura, the suit-shirt that covers the men from tip to toe, how clean and pressed it looks all the time. She wouldn't like me to go

Arab on her: sounds like too much ironing.

Not on dates alone do they live here. There's a staggering variety of food available. We bring Leo out for a Polynesian meal. Half naked women are dancing in what appears to be a Tahitian style, being watched by some modestly clothed Dubai women who are half shocked, half excited by the display.

Russian whores … Back to the hotel for a nightcap. Leo notices it immediately. Are we innocent or something? Most of the ladies playing up to the well-heeled Arabs are Russian prostitutes. The things you don't read about in the official guidebooks.

An Arab smokes a cigar, clutching a glass of Jameson, two whores on tow. What in the name of the Prophet is going on here? Is Islam crumbling? There's an English band playing. One of the singers smiles as she sings Hotel California. Is she as false as her smile? I shouldn't judge people. She's probably very nice. Butter (even made from camel's milk) wouldn't melt in her mouth.

I ask myself, is the Mid-Atlantic 'culture', so stoutly defended by Bush and Blair in their war, infecting the Arabs? I look at one of these creatures. I notice the sandals he's wearing. His foot isn't tapping to the music. Not even his big toe budges. He must still be an Arab at heart, praise and thanks be to Allah. But if I come back and he's here in ten years time, will he have been sucked in by then? Maybe his little toe will be moving, ever so slightly? And what's going to happen to the prostitutes when younger girls replace them? I must come back some day, as a Colonel in the Salvation Army.

Another lobster … Tomorrow we're going to meet an old acquaintance of Eithne, Neasa McDonagh, a Galwegian, for an Italian lunch. You'll find the Irish everywhere. We tried to catch her earlier but she had a pressing engagement—organising a Christian Doctrine class for her son.

There's an ashtray in front of me in the lobby of the Howard Johnson. I'm relaxing, reading The Mystic Masseur by V. S. Naipaul, a very pleasant novel set in the Hindu community of Trinidad. (In a few days time he turns out to be this year's Nobel Laureate). Opposite me sits a dour Arab. We glance at each other suspiciously. I'm reminded of my first trip to the Gaeltacht, to improve my Irish. Should I say something? Will I be understood? Should I say a few words in English? Or should I retreat to my own little world, the world of books and fantasy? I am rudely awakened.

'No swimming,' he says. Is this some philosophical comment, or a command, or what? I place a cigarette between my lips. 'No wimming!' comes the admonishment, louder. What is he trying to say? No women? He gestures. Is he waving or drowning? 'No swimming!' he says again. 'Not good!'

May the fleas of a thousand camels infect your armpits, I say, in Munster Irish. I light a cigarette. The Arab springs to his feet. Crikey! What have I landed myself in now? He moves swiftly to another table. I breathe a sigh of relief and attempt to read another page or two of the novel. The Chinese say that one must chew a book to squeeze the juice out of it but I'm not going to have much luck today. I raise my head. He is still staring at me, sourly. Or maybe he's in love with me? Or is it that he hates me and all the whities of the earth? I light another cigarette. The nerves, you know. Lawrence of Arabia then stands up and in a minute he is gone.

'And may Allah go with you,' I say, in whispered tones.

My imagination is running riot. I can't concentrate on the novel. Its humour no longer infects me. Is your man going to return, this time with a khanjar, a long sharp dagger? Weapons have I none, except a pen. Is the pen mightier than the khanjar?

We have lunch with Neasa McDonagh in the Emirates Tower, one of the fanciest hotels in the world. It's not going to be easy facing the poverty we are likely to encounter in Mumbai, our next stop.

Defence Minister AWOL … The hotel, and a few more, is owned by Sheikh Mohammed, a well-known name at home among the horsey community. He's also the country's Defence Minister, God love him. He obviously thinks the Emirates are safe from attack because when this post-9/11 'war' broke out, he was competing in an equestrian event in Perugia, Italy. He won. (Need you ask?)

His hobbies are more important than any war and maybe that's the way it should be.

Neasa tells us there are about 400 Irish families in Dubai. She doesn't get to know many of them because as soon as you do, they are off again. Wild geese.

Rodeo …. So far we've had nearly four accidents in our taxi from Mumbai Airport. The scariest one was the motorbike that came too close. What was he trying to do, rob us at 60 miles per hour? The scream of scratched metal as curses and prayers mingled in one uproar. I can't understand how the motorcyclist wasn't torpedoed head over heels into eternity. Some kind of rodeo technique for staying glued to the saddle, I expect. Then he veered off into a pre-dawn smudge with a rattle and a roar.

Let's have a look at Namita Devidaya's business column in the Bombay Times. Seems there are thousands of ladies working in Mumbai without their own office toilet. (I didn't see the story covered in any of the Irish-language newspapers to which I subscribe). These good ladies must go out and find a hotel if they want to find relief or otherwise have resource to 'ancient yogic retentive techniques' as she says. I suppose it's different with men, where there's a willy there's a way.

Namita tells us of a moving incident. One woman, lucky enough to have a fully equipped office, betook herself to the place of refuge only to see a sign outside the toilet, OFFICE SPACE—TO LET. And there would be no shortage of applications. Bad enough as some of our landlords are, we haven't quite plumbed those depths yet.

Exploding god population … A few hours sleep… As soon as we hit the streets again we are accosted by a fine strapping woman who is our self-appointed guide for the morning. Neither Eithne nor myself have developed a reliable refusal technique as of yet. Something we must learn. Our guide perceives immediately that I'm not a business man and that my interests incline towards the metaphysical, because she instantly proclaims, as though commenting on the weather, that there are 39,000,000 gods in Mumbai alone. (That's a lot, considering there are only 10,000,000 people). Eithne is not impressed with these statistics. It's good that one of us, at least, is not too impressionable.

Mumbai
rags on the pavement –
a body stirs in them

'Behold,' says our guide, pointing to a mangy dog, 'God in dog. Look, God in cat!'

Gods chasing each other. What a strange world, I say to myself. I think of the great bhakti poet Basavanna whom I first encountered in that priceless anthology Speaking of Shiva (Penguin Classics): 'The pot is a god./ The winnowing fan is a god/. The stone in the street is a god./ The comb is a god…gods, gods, there are so many/ there's no place left/for a foot…' Marvelous.

I could follow this guide for an eternity as she introduces me to her pantheon. But she has another schedule in mind for us.

The snake and the milk … I see a snake charmer on his hunkers by the side of the road. A little shrimp of a fellow, may the 39,000,000,000 gods look down on him. Has he been sitting there for the past thousand years, without blinking? Have we now stirred him from a long swoon? He welcomes us.

'God in snake,' says our merry guide, predictably. And in snake charmer too, I wonder? He lifts the lid from his basket. The twisting head of a king cobra emerges and lunges at its owner. A passing beggar pats the snake lovingly on the head and addressing us in his native language he says, I imagine, that the snake's poison has been drained and that we need not fear it.

This was not part of the snake charmer's routine at all. 'Off with you, you good-for-nothing!' he says to the tramp, or words to that effect, breaking his thousand-year old vow of silence. We take a photo of this frazzled fakir and I give him a ten rupee note for his troubles.

'Under no circumstances!' says our guide, preventing me. 'He'll only drink the money. Come, let us buy milk for the snake.'

Excellent idea, I say to myself. Milk for the snake. Do snakes drink milk? We follow her. Holding up her hand she stops the traffic with one wave of her hand, like your man in the song The Mountains of Mourne. I notice that there's a crowd following us by now. It's a procession. Eithne is feeling a little wary. We find ourselves outside a shop, looking in to the shop, looking behind us and all around us at a motley crew of hangers on.

'Milk for the snake, if you please,' I say, rather nonchalantly, to the shopkeeper. He looks at me. He looks at the crowd and at our stout, indefatigable guide. The curse of Saint Patrick on all of this, I say to myself. Two teenagers begin to take down a large bag of powdered milk from the topmost shelf. Ninety rupees. I give them a hundred. I don't bother with the change. I hand the bag of powdered milk to the snake charmer. Job done. He looks at the bag. At this stage I'm beginning to lose the plot. It's not some kind of Fool's Day in Mumbai, is it? The snake charmer looks at the bag from every angle. Remember, there was no plastic around a thousand years ago so maybe he doesn't know what it is. A bag of gold?

'Follow me!' says our leader. Eithne looks at me. 'What's going on?' she asks, a slight tremor in her voice.

'I've no idea in the wide world,' I say.

Next thing you know we find ourselves in a craft emporium. Textiles. Jewellery. The treasures of the Orient. Our guide has vanished, as though swallowed by a giant cobra. We are given a seat before we know where we are and our dry throats are soon being soothed by hot herbal tea. Our senses slowly revive after all the hullabaloo and confusion of a few moments ago. The owner has commenced on an incredible spiel and we are the target of his ornate arrows of speech. I quickly explain (in case it may not be apparent) that I am not a business man, that we are on a tight budget, I am a mere bard from the Isle of

Saints and Scholars. But this fellow out-bards me at every turn. He could sell milk to a cow, as the Hindus say.

As we admire a world of glistening objects, he manages to find out from Eithne what precious and semi-precious stones she likes, what colours—dammit, at this stage he knows more than I do. He has guessed her star sign too. Is he reading her mind? Anyway, the poetry starts pouring out of him:

'Madam, look, if you will, at this amethyst. Did your lustrous eye ever behold anything with which such a delicate shape can be compared, and such colouring!'

We had to admit it was extraordinarily beautiful. Were we being hypnotised? He gazes at me soulfully, then his melting brown eyes rest wistfully on the jewel before looking up into Eithne's eyes and finally he plunges deep into his own soul.

'I will make of this amethyst a necklace for your wife,' he says to me, 'and upon my soul you will not be able to imagine her joy today, tomorrow and the next day, such happiness will it bring to her heart for all days to come.'

I could not deny my wife such joy but she herself cautions me not to disintegrate under the gaze of this Svengali. The price frightens us. Another sup of tea is required. (Whiskey would be even better). This amethyst in the shape of an eye has us both bewitched by now. But a little niggling doubt still remains. Might there be something in the tea? Saint Brendan of the Voyages, come to our assistance, we beg of you. The amethyst hath us in thrall.

A little notebook rests in front of him. This is the battleground. We scribble a figure. He looks at it and scribbles another figure. After a while it looks like an arithmetic exercise book. Back and forth. Ping pong.

Eventually we get it for half price, almost, and we feel elated. The Battle of the Amethyst is over. We emerge as victors. In a broken voice he tells us that he has made no profit whatsoever on the deal but because of the global crisis and since we are his first customers today—a sign of good fortune—the bargain is made. And I suppose our guide will get a few rupees too, wherever she is.

As Irish speakers we are glad to see the Anglicised versions of names being replaced by native forms but as Christopher de Bellaigue explains, it's not quite that simple:

> Once India had a liberal city called Bombay. Its businessmen were cannier than those of the rest of socialist India, its rich more cosmopolitan, its cricketers more flamboyant. Bombay's was a relatively pluralistic tradition, too. In faraway Calcutta, India's British colonizers had spent the nineteenth century creating a paternalistic seat of empire with heavy-handed imitations of English buildings. In Bombay, on the other hand, prosperous native business men collaborated with their foreign masters to create a port city whose architecture amalgamated with appropriate symbolism, European and Indian styles. Well into the 1990s it was possible to explain, as many did, the incidence of the city's povery and corruption as the natural concomitants of Bombay's commercial dynamism …
>
> (India: A Mosaic)

lullaby of ships in Mumbai Bay

sleeping waifs

entwined as one

And what happened? How are things now? The author takes a less than sanguine view on matters:

> Now, India has an ugly, disturbing shrine city called Mumbai. It is a Hindu shrine, since the diverse, generally tolerant religion practised by four out of five Indians has acquired a venomous political identity in the very city where religious minorities like Muslims, the Jains and the Parsees have tended to do best. Officially, Bombay turned into Mumbai in 1996, when the Hindu nationalist government of the state of Maharashtra decided to rename the state capital in the Marathi vernacular. But the context for this semantic shuffle was a rejection of the secular,

universalist values espoused by Mohandas K. Gandhi and Jawaharlal Nehru …

If he's saying that politics and religion should be divorced, then I agree. It took us a long time ourselves to achieve such separation of church and state.

Kerala, here we come … We travel south to Trivandrum, in Kerala, and a car awaits us at the airport, a white Ambassador, to bring us to Somatheeram, a beach resort, nine kilometres from Kovalam. It's a famous Ayurvedic clinic, practising India's traditional medicine. This is our first real destination. Everything up to now has been mere stops on the way.

We move into a thatched cottage, No. 202. It's built according to the principles of traditional architecture, Vasthusilpa. It's not a thatch of straw or reeds, of course, but coconut leaves. Forms to be filled out first. Do you believe in God? How often do you go to the toilet? The basics! And lots more. Do you experience thirst a lot? (Hey, we're Irish). Do you prefer sweet foods to sour and so on and so forth. This is to determine our dosha or constitutional type and Ayurvedic treatments will commence on the following day.

Will I have to drink urine? Ayurveda as offered here has been slightly tailored to suit Western expectations and a good thing too because from some preliminary reading (though I may have jumped in at the deep end), it might otherwise be a bit of a shock to the system. Camel's milk (ustra payas), for instance, is recommended for flatulence. Eyes dimming somewhat? See clearly again with hasti payas, elephant's milk. Otherwise, dab a little breast milk (yes, human) on the eyes with a cotton bud.

What about cow's milk? Not to be drunk after sundown, unless you're a child. Warm goat's milk stirred with a wooden stick is an aphrodisiac.

It used to be said in Ireland, 'An rud ná leigheasfash im nó fuisce níl leigheas air': what butter or whiskey can't cure, can't be cured. Then they told us butter wasn't too good for us. But butter is highly prized in India, in its clarified form as ghee.

I don't suppose you ever had a swig of urine? Cow's urine won't do you a bit of harm—indeed, it strengthens the mind. (Of course, the author, publisher, printer, distributor, bookseller etc. of this book is not responsible for any adverse reactions to treatments).

Goat's or sheep's urine for asthma. Donkey's urine for mental diseases. The mare is best but the stallion might do in an emergency.

Eithne's father, Dr. Seán Ó Cléirigh, was a pioneer in the field and studied Ayurveda in India. He would be happy to see us here today. What a pity he didn't live to realize his dream of opening an Ayurvedic clinic in Dublin. He was a mover and shaker when TM came to Ireland. I got involved too. I once saw a letter addressed to him as Minister for Immortality. I jest not.

So, we knew a thing or two already about Ayurverda and what's in store: the massages, the oils and the medicaments from herbs grown lovingly here in Somatheeram.

Meanwhile, looking around, we are in agreement that we have reached Paradise. Terrace after terrace of cottages down to the Arabian Sea, fishermen out all hours, day and night, light breezes through palm fronds, flowers of vivid hue, of every shape, the odd hen scratching the sand, a kitten on the lookout for vermin, frogs meditating in the shade, noisy insects exuding life, ants running about on secret missions, colourful butterflies being blown this way and that by sea breezes in the luminous evening air… but over and above everything else, the tooth-filled smiles of Kerala folk, bless them.

Everywhere the hucksters, even on the beach. Selling scarves. A boy says hello. He says he's seventeen but he doesn't look like he's in his teens yet. I mistakenly think he's begging. He is insulted when I say I didn't bring any rupees with me. He stands back, in shock.

'I am not looking for rupees,' he says, 'I just want to talk to you about soccer.' Wrong guy. The quiz team from the Irish Village in Dubai, that's who you want. We change the subject to something I might know a little more about, films.

golden-draped, statuesque
a woman walks
the sands of a thousand years

Have I seen Titanic? Sure. He smiles. We have something in common. But I put my foot in it again. What would you like to be when you're big? A fisherman? A fisherman is it, his eyes seem to say, what kind of a bloke are you? He's going to be a doctor, an Ayurvedic doctor. What else!

Night falls without any warning. Waves and insects are loud again. Somatheeram is peaceful but not all of Kerala enjoys such peace. I read in a newspaper, The Hindu, that the Minister for Backward Classes [sic] is examining tribal claims for extra land and employment opportunities. The first thing he's got to do is change the name of his ministry, don't you think?

Caw-caw …. Keralan crows are a cheeky lot. Last night we were given a big plate of fruit containing grapes and a red banana. We kept some for breakfast. Crows joined us for a bite, vociferous in demanding their rights. They took a particular interest in the small grapes. Their modus operandi was to pinch a bunch of grapes and then pick each grape, singly, squirreling them away under the coco-nut leaves of the awnings and in flower pots. Was this for a rainy day? No, they would be eaten on the spot now, in comparative privacy, before some other hungry mouth or beak comes along.

I thought of a story I had read years before concerning the sage, Ramana Maharshi. Some of his followers had been throwing stones at a crow. The sage put a stop to this carry on. He had recognised the crow: some poor soul that had reincarnated as a bird. When in the course of time the bird died, a memorial was built to it. That's my memory of what happened but I could just as easily have imagined it.

One way or the other, I think crows are wonderful, especially Máire Ní Dhálaigh (Mary Daly), the crow that finds itself trailing all the others as they go home to roost. I like the respect shown to animals and birds in the Gaelic tradition of naming them: Donncha an Chaipín (Donough of the Cap, the cock stonechat), Jónaí an Scrogaill (Joan of the Long Neck, the heron), Máirín an Chlúimh (Hairy Maureen, the caterpillar), an t-einín beannaithe (the sacred bird, the wagtail, an bhóín Dé (God's little cow, the ladybird).

fireflies in a dream –
fishing-boat lanterns playing
out at sea

There are many sacred groves in Kerala. Over a thousand. Until recently they remained unperturbed, just as one would not contemplate bulldozing a lios, or fairy fort, in Ireland. This respectful attitude has helped preserve the ecosystem here. Whatever progress is to be made by Keralans, and I wish them good luck and prosperity, it would be unfortunate for the ecosystem, for the food chain and for ecotourism, if that insight was lost.

The Naga … Great respect is due to the snake-god, in Kerala and in other parts of India. (The Sanskrit word naga and the Irish word nathair would seem to be related). Large areas were set aside so that the naga could enjoy its freedom. With huge demand on land, scientists and rationalists are trying their best to discredit superstitions, if superstition is the correct word; however, the best scientists understand that certain traditions must be upheld.

The other night a local flautist paid us a visit and he played a merry tune in honour of the Nagaraja, King of the Snakes. Listening to him, I knew that composer Seán Ó Riada wasn't far wrong when he linked ancient Irish music to the music of India. There are many other links between the two cultures, as

Joseph Lennon has shown us in his book Irish Orientalism. We could look at law and literature, myth and hagiography for a start.

midnight
emits its sacred snort,
Manannán's horses

Is not our sacred river, the Boyne (an Bhóinn) linguistically cognate with Govinda, a popular name for Krishna; and was it not two cows from India which nourished Eithne (no, another Eithne) on the banks of the Boyne in mythical times? Ní bréag í an fhírinne, the truth is not a lie!

Who knows how many animals, birds, insects and reptiles live in these sacred groves or visit them—the frog, the lizard, the ant, the snail, the earthworm, the crow, the owl, the parrot greener than green tea, the humming bird that hums all morning, the bee, the butterfly; rats, mice, squirrels, hares and their friends all help with the scattering of seeds and fruits. No wonder scientists say that there are only ten natural paradises left on this earth and Kerala is one of them. Floreat!

But a new generation is growing up now and their faith is not as firm as that of their ancestors. Many of the sacred groves are endangered, more is the pity; medicinal plants are being plundered and land for building or for cultivation is keenly sought after. If this miraculous ecosystem declines, no one can predict the effect on every link of this chain. Think what you like about worshiping snakes … superstition, sorcery, animism, shamanism, paganism, whatever; nature will suffer, conservation will suffer if this belief system goes. Chomh cinnte is ata púdar i nDoire: as sure as there's gunpowder in Derry.

It is often mistakenly assumed that the name Kerala comes from kera (the soft coconut); the books that I've read provide another etymology for this word, however. The prefix cher means "additional" or "extra" and this land is an additional piece of land which was once submerged beneath the Arabian Sea, an area now home to American aircraft carriers. Most likely, it is a sliver of land recovered from the sea as a consequence of the earth's volcanic or seismic activity.

This is an ancient country where dolmens dot the landscape, reminding one of megalithic relics of home. Has anyone undertaken any comparative research on our mutual heritages?

Diverse religions have always existed side by side in Kerala. The Apostle known as Doubting Thomas brought Christianity to this place in the year 52 A.D. and Thomas is still a common name in these parts.

There are about 15,000 Ayurvedic healers practicing in Kerala today, believe it or not, 15,000 souls who collect healing plants and medicines and who produce salves for export. I recall Cyril Ó Céirín , the author of Wild and Free—may be rest in peace –and his wife Kit and their awareness of the secrets of our hedgerows. How we've disregarded all that and our own valuable healing tradition.

Brahmi…When I consulted them in Somatheeram these doctors could tell that I was a bit nuts. Too many thoughts circling the mind at any one time, too much to remember, the 39,000,000 gods we'd left behind in Mumbai included. The doctors gave me some blue pills to take, tablets which included 28 different varieties of herb, brahmi amongst them. On top of this, the most principal healer prepared a paste, also made of brahmi, a medicinal remedy for the central nervous system. I even managed to get hold of a giant of a book, an enormous compendium outlining the diversity of Ayurvedic herbs that are used in this area. Ah…it's listed there too, that same brahmi! Of course, if you're a herbalist, you'll know this herb by its Latin name—Bacopa monnieri. This herb is described as being an elixir for the brain; it may also be used for epilepsy. I've been known to have brainstorms that have been so stormy as to lift me off my feet. A brahmi defecit, wouldn't you say?

I like the story about the Ayurvedic student, Jivaka. Before being accepted as a student he and his companions were sent out to seek plants which had no medicinal properties whatsoever. His companions came back that evening with a little bundle of what they thought to be useless plants. Jivaka did not return, nor did he return the following day. When he eventually returned, he said to Dvarapala, the gatekeeper, 'I could find nothing that did not have some value.' Massage … We're advised on what to eat and what to avoid. An hour and a half of massage every day, two technicians working in synchronised fashion. Then it's time for thaila dhara, warm oil dripping on your forehead. Being well-oiled in Kerala means something else at home - a Thiarna an Domhain is a Rí na Cruinne ('Lord of the Earth and King of the Universe' as my mother used to say)! Actually, her Irish was corrupt and she used to say 'A Rí na Tine' (King of Fire).

Easter Rising … Have you read A Suitable Boy by Vikram Seth? Do. It's only 1,474 pages long. There's a passage in which a junior lecturer attempts to put James Joyce on his reading list. The professor is not too happy with this suggestion. 'This kind of writing is unhealthy for our students,' he says. I was interested in finding out if any of our Irish poets are taught in Indian schools and I bought An Anthology of English Poems that is aimed at second-year students studying for a B.A./B.Sc, published by Gautam Publications, Calicut. I paid 15 rupees for it. It contains a dozen poems. One of them is Easter 1916 by Yeats. One could see why the poem might appeal to Indians. We shared the little problem of how to turf the English out. Well, if they have thrown the English out they have let them in the back door because I have yet to see a bookshop which hasn't the likes of P.G. Wodehouse sitting beside Aurobindo; though educated in Britain, Aurobindo was a freedom fighter before turning his back on conflict to pursue a life of poetry, yoga and contemplation in the French enclave of Pondicherry. Irish Theosophists influenced his thinking.

Anyway, what information are we given about Yeats? 'He was born in Irelarrd,' it would seem and he was 'in love with Malld Gorlas.' Nobody, least of all a poet, could fall in love with a Malld Gorlas. Unless brahmi quietens me down considerably, I think I will lodge a complaint.

We visit a large, wooden palace, a national treasure, Padmanabhapuram, in Thuckalay. Among many treasures is the king's bed, a "Medicinal Cot" which the Dutch East India Company presented to the king, a cot fashioned from 64 different types of Ayurvedic timber. The dragon motif is common on much of the furniture in these parts, a vestige of the trading that was once frequent between Kerala and China.

We are trying to learn some of the local language, phrases such as nandhi for "thank you" and nale kannam for "I'll see you tomorrow". Nearly every foreigner here seems to speak German or English. Why do so few people bother to learn local languages?

We head south again towards Kanyakumari and find ourselves leaving Kerala behind. Now we are in the neighbouring state of Tamil Nadu, the territorial boundaries of which were re-drawn in the 1950s, based on linguistic divisions. Three different seas come together in this region, the Arabian Sea, the Indian Ocean and the Bay of Bengal, and the differences between each of the three can be perceived in the colour of the tides. Together, they create a new colour, the colour of the amethyst that we bought from Svengali the other day. I hope he had a second customer.

People come to the place we are in now from far and wide. They come to watch the beauty of the sunrise and the sunset, such is their spectacular beauty. There is a memorial to Gandhi here too, in the place where his ashes were laid for a time. The memorial has a special opening in its roof so that the sun's rays can shine through annually on the anniversary of Gandhi's birth, the second of October. An incredibly-tall statue celebrates the legacy of another famous public figure, the poet Thiruvalluvar, who lived in the second century. When will Ireland erect a five hundred foot statue in honour of our first poet Aimhirghin Glúngheal?

These memorials and monuments aren't what fascinates me about this place, however. More interesting is the fact that it was here where Vivekananda first saw the imprint of the goddess; it was here too that he spent a period in contemplation before setting out for America and the Parliament of Religions which took place in Chicago on the eleventh of September, 1893, an event which triggered my imagination the first time I heard tell of it. Vivekananda was the pioneer who brought the spirituality of India to the West. The branches of that spiritual tree survive even if the visionary who planted its roots has passed on. Everything in Swami Vivekanada's writings was soma or nectar for me when I studied them first, all of thirty years ago. I was young and idealistic back then! I never forgot what I saw in his writings, however. They made a great impact on me at the time. Diabetes killed him in the end. In the absence of any cure for that disease, he died when he was just forty years of age.

Vivekanada outlined a unique vision of the world, one which was real rather than abstract, a vision born from long hours of study, contemplation, struggle and self-doubt. This vision of his was as a shining torch for him, from the very first moments his master Ramakrishna opened his eyes to the truth. On reading Vivekanada and other Indian sages, I knew I had a soulmate (anamchara) in him (and in India), someone who would accompany me through the vicissitudes of life.

Even as a young man Vivekanada seems to have been a gifted individual, a thoughtful person who was both fun-loving and well-read. He read the big philosophers of the West, Schopenhauer, Hume and Kant, while simultaneously embarking on his own mystical journey. He had the nature of the true mystic and seems to have had many revelations during the course of his short life, whether in the solitude of nature or when traversing the worlds between time and space.

For a while Vivekananda associated with a group of philosophical students who were endeavouring to move Hinduism in the direction of Reason and its precepts. He met the great master Ramakrishna at this point, however, and the encounter caused him to change philosophical direction. From this pivotal encounter emerged newer and deeper insights into the nature of his own being. From that point on, he embarked on a much more dramatic and exciting journey, a voyage of the soul which was far more important than any philosophical convention or trip to America. Once he came to an understanding of his own nature, he predicted that he would leave this world behind, and this is exactly how his life turned out. When he achieved that stage of self-realization, he duly died.

One day, his Master was in a state of ecstasy, a state which (if the Latin explanation—ex stare—is accurate) means to stand outside oneself. Ramakrishna happened to touch Vivekananda and a divine, electrical contact occurred. Vivekananda immediately entered a similarly ecstatic state whereby it was possible for the Master to discern the development of his pupil's soul.

Let us sit back and enjoy some of Vivekananda's inspiring rhetoric, a rhetoric which helped the people of the West gain an insight into the soul of India. Not only did his words inspire the people of the West to develop new attitudes towards the East; given that Vivekananda was writing at a time when his people were under the yoke of foreign domination, his words also served to inspire his own countrymen and women:

> I will try to present before you the secret of India, what India means. If those whose eyes have been blinded by the glamour of material things, whose whole dedication of life is to eating and drinking and enjoying, whose ideal of possession is lands and gold, whose God is money, and whose goal is a life of ease and comfort in this world and death after that, whose minds never look forward, and who rarely think of anything higher than the sense objects in the midst of which they live; such as these go to India, what do they see? Poverty, squalor, superstition, darkness, hideousness everywhere. Why? Because in their minds enlightenment means dress, education, social politeness. Whereas Occidental nations have used every effort to improve their material position, India has done differently. There live the only men in the world, who, in the whole history of humanity, never went beyond their frontiers to conquer anyone else, who never coveted that which belonged to anyone else, whose only fault was that their lands were so fertile, and they accumulated wealth by the hard labour of their hands, and so tempted other nations to come and despoil them. They are content to be despoiled, and to be called barbarians, and in return, they want to send to this world visions of the Supreme, to lay bare for the world the secrets of human nature, to rend the veil that conceals the real man, because they know the dream, because they know that behind this materialism lives the real divine nature of man which no sin can tarnish, no crime can spoil, no lust can taint; which fire

cannot burn, nor water wet, which cannot dry, nor death kill ..."
(Karma Yoga and Bhakti Yoga)

These are profound sentiments, echoing Matthew 6.19-24. Unsurprisingly, when the Americans heard rhetoric such as this, they began to ask themselves the question, "Why the hell are we giving money to missionaries and sending them out to India?" Some of the missionaries were afraid that their "raison d'etre" would be undermined and a propaganda campaign was initiated against Vivekananda. History shows that that particular campaign proved fruitless. On returning to India, Vivekananda was welcomed by enthusiastic crowds wherever he went. He was one of the first Indian revivalists and therefore one of the country's first Nationalists also. He advised the people of India to forget about all of the gods—(remember, the 39,000,000 gods and their agents who were ready to grab me in Mumbai?): "The only god who is awake—is that of our own Indian race—their hands everywhere, their feet everywhere, their ears everywhere. India includes all of us and every living thing. All of the gods are asleep…" I don't know whether any other scholars have noted this yet, but these are the same sentiments as were expressed by Tagore in a poem of his that goes as follows:

Leave this chanting and singing and telling of beads!
Whom dost thou worship in this lonely dark
corner of a temple with doors all shut?
Open thine eyes and see thy God is not before thee!
He is there where the tiller is tilling the hard ground
and where the pathmaker is breaking stones.
He is with them in the sun and in shower, and his garment is covered in dust.
(Rabindranath Tagore: An Anthology)

Now that I think about it, it was from Swami Vivekananda that I really learned about religion for the first time. I was raised as a Catholic but when a priest once refused to listen to my Confession, I lost interest in the rituals of Catholicism—particularly when the Catholic Church abandoned the use of Latin and suppressed

Liberation Theology. Just in case you are worried, I hadn't murdered anybody or anything like that. It was only that I said to him at one point—"Please absolve me quickly, Father, because I am not even sure that I believe I have sinned here—or whether this sacrament is having any effect on me." I lost my religious belief at that point but it returned to me again once I read Vivekananda. This time I believed in all things, in all religions even; I wouldn't let the minor points of doctrine or ritual come between me and realization again.

Christians were annoyed with Vivekananda when he advised his followers not to seek repentance for their sins. (It is still a matter of some debate of course what John the Baptist meant by his use of the word "teshuvah"; it is likely that "repentance" isn't the exact meaning in this case; what it really means is "return"—return to the roots of your own true nature, Self or soul. Vivekananda advised his followers not to let the weight of sin (so-called) drag them down or prevent them from seeking a true insight into their own human nature—a nature that is untainted at its core. Those words of his set me free. They also inspired me to write poems which would express the happiness associated with this sense of freedom—and poems and rhymes for young people as well.

Vivekananda viewed the world as "leelah", a place for God's play and entertainment. We should not constantly seek answers to all of our questions. Why this? Why that? Why death? It is all a divine game, according to Vivekananda, a game which we should enthusiastically partake in. We should be joyful fellow-players with the Lord. It isn't logical to seek reasons for everything. Why was the world created? If you really need an answer to this question, then you are only limiting the reality of God. Vivekananda was dubious whether a historical personage known as Jesus Christ had ever existed. Historians of his day, including Josephus and Philo, listed a range of sects which were operating at this time but there is no mention of Christ except for one ambiguous reference which may or may not be accurate.

It is strange, in a way, that Vivekananda questioned Christ's existence. Did he not know of the strong tradition which claims that Jesus Christ lived in India—after his Resurrection, and still known in India as Issa. (How close to Irish

Íosa!). The great teacher Osho, once dubbed the most dangerous man on earth, says in his book Glimpses of a Golden Childhood that it was while living in the Himalayas that some of the great sages ended their days.

> It is where Lao Tzu died. In the valleys of the Himalayas Buddha died. Jesus died. Moses died. No other mountains can claim Moses, Jesus, Lao Tzu, Buddha, Bodhidharma, Milarepa, Marpa, Tilopa, Naropa...

Remember all of those names now in case you ever find yourself taking part in a table quiz in the Irish Village in Dubai.

Vivekananda's importance lies in the fact that he had a great understanding of the unbroken Vedic tradition in India and that the revival of that tradition was analogous with the revival of the Indian nation itself. He hated the aping of colonial ways that had taken place in India when it was part of the British Empire. Ultimately, his gospel was a gospel of love. Concepts such as friendship, fondness, love, empathy, respect and desire etc.—these are all unique and separate from one another, in our way of thinking. Christians think of "love of God" as being accurate enough as a blanket term to convey their belief. But love of God was a vague concept in the tradition I was raised in. What does it mean exactly? To keep God's commandments and to be kind to the neighbours? And who are my neighbours? Are the Afghans my neighbours? They certainly are.

The Hindu approaches this whole question in much the same way as a scientist does, breaking the question down into its separate components. The love of God which the Christian espouses (unless he/she is a mystic or a Saint Francis who bumped into Shamz of Tabriz) does not cater for separate categories—as far as I know. It is the same concept from one Sunday to the next. The level of its intensity is always the same. Vivekananda's famous thesis Bhakti Yoga, The Yoga of Love and Devotion provides detailed descriptions of the different forms of divine love which exist. It begins with Shanta, which is a gentle and peaceful form of love akin to friendship—the trust and confidence which two friends have in one another and the enjoyment they take in one another's company. This stage of divine love is analogous with that of the Bhakta who has reached a particular stage in his spiritual evolution. After this comes Vatsalya, a form of love wherein the deity is not perceived as the dominant father-figure but as a child of our own. For a similar analogy, think of Saint Ita in her desert sanctuary when she "adopted" the baby Jesus. (There are big similarities between the Irish hagiographic tradition and the Indian one. If there weren't, I might never have taken an interest in this subject).

The highest point in this remarkable Bhakti tradition is termed Madhura when each and every person is transformed into a woman, a woman who is in love with her sweet Lord. Every human being taking the form of a woman and lavishing her love on the Beloved, awaiting his kisses! And that is it; that is the tradition in a nutshell! If we love the Divine it must be completely and unconditionally.

What is provided above is just a brief outline of some of Vivekananda's teachings, some of the beliefs which are found in the Indian traditions of bhakti and Advaita. Vivekananda, the wandering monk who helped re-invigorate self-pride and national feeling amongst his fellow countrymen and who paved the way for Gandhi and the development of the new Indian nation, the republic that is India today.

And here I am standing on the rock known as Vivekananda's Rock; down below me three beautiful seas kiss one another. Vivekananda's name will never be forgotten nor that of his Master. Explore them!

Tomorrow, the 15th of October, we will fly from Trivandrum to New Delhi. We will sail down the Ganges with the help of Mother Ganga and if all goes well, we will return to Delhi again.

Mo chúig chéad slán leat! (Five hundred farewells!) I leave behind a piece of my heart with you, Kerala! I will have to return here some day if possible to recover it. May every good wish be upon you, Kerala—on your rice, on your tea, on your coffee, on your rubber, on your pepper, on your nuts and on all of your fruits.

Good look with the fishing!

Away with the Moon, crackers!

There is a red-legged partridge here known as the chakor. This bird stares endlessly at the moon, without blinking. Valuable bird-lore or ornithology or what? Lore or science? India is a land of science. It makes no difference what prefix you add to the 'ology'—this country encapsulates every form of science: mythology, sexology, ornithology etc. Taken together they form a universal body of scientific knowledge, all part of the interlinking chain of being, of life itself. For the last 10,000 years, the people of India have succeeded in fishing for everything under the sun with nets divine. The same was true of all great civilisations, our own included, an era before the myths began to be collected and written down. Culture changed then and became just another artefact; it became museumified, so to speak. From then on, you had to read a book to discover the myths. Before that you just had to look at the natural world around you.

In India, the myths jump out at you. They are not all corralled into libraries and museums yet; they are not archived away in the Department of Folklore. In India, mythology still lives and breathes and dances. It laughs and shouts and stares between the two eyes at you. It peers out from stone and wood. It is in the air. Here myth is both ancient and living. It is in front of you and behind you and there is always a new myth awaiting you around the corner.

You have between now and 2016…It is not so long ago since the same wonderful and ancient approach to life as can be found in India was also prevalent in Ireland, when a special lore was associated with every lake, river and hill. Ask a teenager in Athlone (Baile Átha Luain/ The Town of the Ford of Luan) who Luan might be and they won't know what you are talking about. This is Ireland of the twenty-first century, a country that is poorer than ever despite the increase in golf-courses. Is the torch of ages quenched? No, I don't think so. I wouldn't be writing these words and in Irish, if such were the case. We may yet build a memorial to Aimhirghin Glúngheal, a statue that reaches to the heavens and with his words (which sound like they've come fresh from the Upanishads):

Am gaeth i m-muir…
I am the wind upon the sea
wave of the ocean
murmur of the billows
ox of the seven combats
vulture upon the rocks
beam of the sun
fairest of plants
wild boar in valour
salmon in the water
lake in the plain
a word of science…

And people might pause a while and look at it with wonder. Indian myths are manifold and there is no escaping them. They are visible everywhere— in music, dance, in craftwork, even in food. Newspaper editorials such as those of The Times of India regularly refer to mythology when debating essential topics relating to Indian society. The festivals, religious and otherwise, also celebrate myths and legends and a slew of gods and goddesses.

There is a mythology relating to trees and flowers. The lotus, a flower which emerges from the mud of the river-bed yet makes no contact with the water, has a mythology all of its own. It is said that the goddess Lakshmi uses a lotus flower as her seat, Lakshmi the goddess of wealth. Compare this with apples and nuts that hang from the trees in Ireland; for the most part, they have almost all lost their mythological resonances and associations.

In Delhi, we stay in a hotel named the Hotel Kanishka; even the names of the hotels here have both history and mythology entwined in them. I think of the names of the hotels in Ireland; the Imperial and the Royal and the like.

The Irish king Guaire was such a generous person that he continued giving to the poor even after he was dead. The Irish saints and the Indian saints teach us that it is better to give away to others in this life than it is to continually store up wealth. An Indian king named Mahavir decided it would be better to give everything he had to the poor and the destitute and then to journey into the unknown. In the end, all he had left was the costly cloak on his back but just as he left the outskirts of the royal city he came across a crippled beggar, a man whose disability had prevented him from reaching the city in time so as to be present for the division of king's possessions. "I am too late, I suppose," the poor unfortunate said, and Mahavir presented him with half of his cloak before hurrying into the wilderness. On his approach to the forest, what remained of Mahavir's cloak became entangled in a rosebush and Mahavir stopped for a moment before trying to free the torn clothing from the tree. He considered his situation and contemplated on the fact that he had now lost everything; he was penniless and completely naked and yet completely free. He had nothing more to burden him., nothing left to worry about, nothing which would come between him and a good night's sleep.

Indian film-makers continue to incorporate the old myths and epics into their works, even in the present-day, whereas we in Ireland will never see the Fiannaíocht (the Fianna Cycle) or the Rúraíocht (the Ulster Epic Cycle) on screen—not until these treasures of our cultural inheritance have been memorized by the young generation and the old great tales re-invented by them. It's that simple, the same radical philosophy which Pearse sought to implement when he founded his school, Scoil Éanna along the lines of Rabindranath Tagore's Shantiniketan. More chivalry than ultra-nationalism in its essence. (Yeats actually put Pearse and Tagore in contact with another).

We settle into the Hotel Kanishka, a hotel run by Sikhs—the turbaned heads of the staff and the taxi-drivers give the game away. Until recently the air in Delhi was heavily-polluted and visitors were advised not to travel by open (three-wheeled) taxi or by rickshaw as to do so would induce a bad bout of coughing and wheezing. I open the Yellow Pages that's on the locker next to the bed where there is the following message from the Minister for Trade:

> The 6th edition of the Directory was very well edited and meticulously planned. I do hope the latest edition would be better than the previous one.

Amen to that! And the eighth edition? Better again than the last, no doubt, and further improvements in store next year and the year after—until a state of yellow nirvana is achieved. Take your own meaning from the Minister's words. That is one thing to enjoy about India; you can interpret anything in the way that you see fit. In a sense, there is no such thing as Hinduism; there are just a multitude of versions of what is deemed to be Hinduism. And somebody else will think of another new version tomorrow.

I rarely complain about anything. You couldn't call me a cranky person, except for when I write the odd letter to the newspaper and that's often tongue in cheek. I made a complaint this afternoon, however, when we opened the rottenest bottle of wine the world has ever seen. The label on the bottle claimed the wine to be Italian and it was expensive enough, going on for one thousand rupees. We had asked for an Indian wine originally, a wine which isn't the easiest to get but which tastes excellent and is priced much more reasonably.

"Take a sup of that there yourself," I said to the restaurant manager. He took a quick slug and grimaced. That's more like cooking sherry than wine, he said. Would you agree with me? he asked. I agreed with him.

Surprise, surprise—what appears next but a bottle of Indian wine—not a full bottle mind. The portion of Italian wine which had been removed was deducted from the new bottle. We had a nice relaxed drink and Eithne was a bit merry after the wine. To be honest, we've taken very little alcohol since the beginning of this trip—we've held religiously to the Ayurvedic diet prescribed for us.

In the newspaper there is a frightening article about eighteen people who died after drinking hooch. Every corner of the world must have its poitín-makers and its own brand of moonshine. They make a nice drink here, a type of "milk" made from nuts. The locals leave this juice at the top of the tree where it ferments. Sometimes, a sloth comes along, and drinks his fill, however. Next thing the poor sloth gets woozy and falls to the ground below in a heap. You get the odd rogue of an elephant who's looking out for a drink too and likes nothing better than a belly full of this same nut-milk. It is better to steer clear of them when they've taken a wee drop of the craythur.

This evening we try a Chinese meal but it turns out to be awful. "Everything OK?" the waiter enquires but I haven't it in me to make another complaint today.

"Where are you from?" he asks.

"Ireland," both of us say, replying simultaneously.

"Ah…Ireland!" he whispers with a mystic voice and places his hand over his heart. It is as if he has assumed an ecstatic state, as if a divine ecstasy has taken hold of him. Who have we here? Ramakrishna II? I'd say that he hasn't a clue really where Ireland is and that if we had said Iceland instead of Ireland, his reaction would have been the same.

Breakfast. A giant of a muscle-man sitting across from us. A Gulf-based American marine? A member of the Special Forces? He has thrown back about five glasses of orange juice already and the waiters are looking over in his direction, sniggering quietly. The Times of India and the English-language newspapers keep us up-to-date with what's happening in the world at large and the big events of the day in this part of Asia. It is pleasing to see Gandhi's words still cited in the media here even in these troubled times. Gandhi and his philosophy are still very much an element within the public consciousness here and they screen the epic film entitled Gandhi annually. The screenings are always on the same date, the second of October, each year. We visited the place where he was cremated, removing our shoes the same as if we were visiting a temple or a mosque. And it is a temple really, this particular memorial. Gandhi was no god but he was certainly a mahatma; atma means "soul", maha means "big", and Gandhi was undoubtedly both—a big soul, a great soul. (In fact, it was Tagore who gave him the name mahatma).

How often do you see an Irish newspaper providing a daily digest of the wisdom of the world's great sages and philosophers? Reading the words of sages might provide solutions to many of the world crises we currently face. In Ireland the culture of respect and reverence was once an essential element of society, the respect and appreciation of the past and the peoples who have preceded us. The disappearance of such a culture of respect makes a nation infinitely poorer. If India teaches us anything, it teaches us this. Who knows? It may well be the Irish language minority who will keep the flames of civilisation alive back home, in terms of respecting ancestral values, insights and lore that still have beauty and relevance.

Every woman in India is a princess in her own right. It doesn't matter whether she's leaving the temple barefoot or down at the ghat washing clothes. I meet Professor Satchidanandan in the Sahitya Akademi (National Academy of Literature) in Delhi. On the wall of his office hangs a historic photo—Gandhi listening to Tagore in Shantiniketan. I'd give all the tea in India to get my hands on that photo—but it's not for sale. Strangely enough, Eithne recognised the Professor upon meeting him. He was on the same flight as we were from Trivandrum. From Kerala originally, the Professor was attending a rally of various tribal peoples in Trivandrum, tribals who were agitating for their civil rights.

Eithne buys a book of short stories by Tagore, the Nobel Prize winner who handed the title "Sir" back to the British after the massacre at Amritsar. Two words which Tagore uses a great deal in his stories and poems are "joyfulness" and "gloominess". As with the Irish "suairceas" and "duairceas" he, too, has the contrasting "s" and the "d" in surke-durke!

Tagore is a writer who is well worth reading. Tagur means Lord and Tagore was actually a landlord, a landlord who had something of a divine appearance about him—at least for those first Europeans who encountered him.

> The contrast between Tagore's commanding presence in Bengali literature and culture and his near-total eclipse in the rest of the world is perhaps less interesting than the distinction between the view of Tagore as a deeply relevant and many-sided contemporary thinker in Bangladesh and India, and his image in the West as a repetitive and remote spiritualist. Graham Greene had, in fact, gone on to explain that he associated Tagore "with what Chesterton calls the 'the bright pebbly eyes' of the Theosophists". Certainly, an air of mysticism played some part in the "selling" of Rabindranath Tagore to the West by Yeats, Pound, and his other early champions. Even Anna Akhmatova, one of Tagore's few

> later admirers (who translated his poems into Russian in the mid-1960s), talks of "that mighty flow of poetry which takes its strength from Hinduism as from the Ganges, and is called Rabindranath Tagore...
>
> (Amartya Sen in India: A Mosaic)

Two Catholics, Chesterton and Greene, mocking the spirituality of the East. They had nothing better to do with their time, I suppose. Thankfully, the influence of both of these writers is on the wane in Ireland somewhat; for years, we practically worshipped these two English writers as demi-gods. And the same people who considered these fine Catholics to be beyond reproach would often have been completely ignorant of our own native prayers in the Gaelic tradition!

A call from the reception desk: "A Dubliner here to see you both." Who is it but the film buff Siraj Zaidi, originally a native of Lucknow.

"What the devil?" I say at this happy surprise.

"I heard from the Embassy that you were visiting the city and I thought I'd say Hello!"

It just shows; you could be anywhere in the world and…!

"And what brought you to Delhi," I ask him.

"A woman," he says, noting the look of surprise on my face. "We met one another via the Internet!" (They have married one another since then).

Life is strange. I have known Siraj for years; he's the person who organises the Indian series of films at the IFC in Dublin. In fact, he once produced one of Tagore's plays in the Writer's Museum, in Dublin. The first time I met Siraj he asked me to translate the Koran into Irish. Unfortunately, I never followed up on this request. (I subsequently found out it would have entailed a few years studying in Cairo). Of course, all of the world's classics, religious and secular, should be available in Irish.

Professor K. Satchidanandan sends me a questionnaire about the Irish language and literature in Irish. I spend an entire night working on my responses to the questionnaire and write a 14-page Introduction in the process. I list all of the different names for the country "Ireland" that can be found in the Irish language, many of them names of goddesses. I mention the Droimeann Donn

Dílis
(a name for Ireland: the lovable, brown, white-backed cow) as part of my summary of Gaelic literature and write the following for the Professor: Can you imagine Matthew Arnold, John Milton or Samuel Taylor Coleridge referring to England as a cow?

It is cultural realities such as this which make Ireland more similar to India than it is to England. We'll be back in Delhi again at some stage and can use the opportunity to explore these issues and others with the Professor in more detail. The Professor tells me that he would like to translate some of my poems into his native language—Malayalam.

I have never seen anywhere quite as "imperial" as the Imperial Hotel here in Delhi. Not that we were staying there—we'd do well to afford one drink in the bar there, the Patiala Peg—the name of which had an Irish input by all accounts. A Maharaja lived here once named Bhupinder Singh. He was the ruler of this state, the state of Patiala. A giant of a man, he was six-and-a-half feet tall and had a prodigious appetite. He was often reputed to eat 24 dozen quail at a single sitting. Mounted on his black Arabian stallion, he must have made an impressive sight. The women of the region were in love with him and he had 365 wives in all. Like the bould Thady Quill he had a great interest in all things sports-related and had his own polo team, a team which never lost a match in all the years he was ruler of the region. He had his own band of special warriors within his army too, a group known as the Nihang. I suppose you could say that they were the Fianna of the Punjab. One of their favourite sports involved planting the skulls of their enemies in the ground and then plucking them up with their spears while racing along on horseback. Both horses and riders would be half-crazy with the drug bhang while they played this mad game. This game, in its more civilized form, became tent pegging. As I say, the maharaja's team was never beaten—mainly because he was so generous to the winners that losing didn't bear thinking about.

One of the maharaja's customs was to challenge the Viceroy's Pride, a team which comprised of Irishmen. As usual, the Maharaja was the soul of hospitality and once the match was over he laid on a great spread of food and drink for all the competitors. Apparently, he was amazed at the way the Irish could "hold" their drink. They could enjoy drinking all night and would still be standing in the morning.

Competition time had come around again and the Maharaja's team were very anxious. If the unthinkable were to happen and they were to lose the game, there was a good chance the Maharaja would ensure the pegs they normally used were replaced with their skulls! They had to come up with a plan to outwit the opposition and so they decided to serve double-measures of whiskey to their Irish opponents at the party the night before the match. While the party was in full swing, they also changed the pins around so that the opposition (i.e. the Irishmen) were given a small set of pegs while the Maharaja's team had a larger set for themselves. Sure enough, the Maharaja's team won one again! The barman in the Imperial Hotel related that story to us. Ever since the famous match, it is the tradition that the whiskey measures given out are always doubles!

The Imperial Hotel, Delhi
sleek cats
out on patrol

Namasté! Indians greet one another using this graceful and holy word. Namasté!—their hands clasped together. This simple benediction is symbolic of one soul recognising another. Contrast this with the tradition of shaking hands as practiced in the West. Shaking hands in the western world is often an ambiguous act at best. It is an act that can often appear meaningless or inconsequential. When the poorest of outcasts salutes you here in India—with a namasté—you and he are one and the same in God's eyes. For a moment, you are both equal in this world; one of you may be wearing a shirt and tie while the other is in rags—

but it is the same blood flowing through your veins, two people one in your ultimate destiny, the same sun that shines and sets for both.

Can any historian or anthropologist tell me when the custom of shaking hands first came to Ireland or what we did before this way of greeting one another became the norm? Could we get rid of this hand-shaking custom in Ireland now or is it too late? Is it too firmly engrained within our culture? Could we not replace it with a kiss? The Irish word for a kiss, póg, comes from pax, peace, the kiss of peace introduced to Ireland by Christians. I still remember well the time I spent living in my father's home region of Schleswig-Holstein, in Germany. The older people there greeted each another in an incredibly formalized manner—shaking hands with a sharp clicking of the heels. Militarism. Extreme Prussianism. Let's put an end to this whole shaking hands business! Did An Craoibhín (Douglas Hyde, the first President of Ireland) make mention of this tradition when he called for Ireland to be de-anglicized? He may have had a point when referring to the bad influence of a foreign style of dress and manners, so let's re-echo his mantra, Down with trousers! (How innocent he and most of his audience were back then).

nothing remains
but the gate:
temple of air

Belly of a goat …The beauty of the carpets from Kashmir. "Look at how soft this wool is," the merchant, Nasir A. Khan says. "Persians from Kashmir made this, they used the belly of a goat…why did they do this do you think?" This is a tough question. I try to think why they might have used the belly-wool of the goat as opposed to any other part of the body. I can't think of a good response to the merchant's query. The answer turns out to be very simple. The wool of the goat's belly is brighter and smoother than any other part of the goat's hair because it is less exposed to the sun than other parts of the body. The goats of Kashmir don't spend their time sunning themselves—bolg le gréin ("belly to the sun") as we say in Irish. This carpet is patterned with a series of windows beyond which the tree of life is growing—the windows are the impressions of what windows might be like, the original design made by nomads who lived in tents.

Nasir instructed his assistant to remove all of the carpets and rugs which were on the floor of the shop in order to spread out a particular rug that had caught our eye. It is necessary to have no distractions and to focus completely on the splendour of this one rug. The deal is eventually done. "That's the end of our purchases, now," we say to ourselves. Eithne is asked to sign her name on the back of the rug so as to ensure that it is the same rug which arrives in Dublin on our return and not some tatty half-brother.

Previous to this, I always though of shopping as a fairly mundane obligation; I've never been able to get excited about curtains and other household items. In India, however, there is an excitement in the buying and selling process that I have never experienced before. There is the ritual of examining each product in all its intricate or simple glory. The pride exhibited by the sellers is infectious and it makes you feel proud as well, privileged to be an element in the ritual of transaction. One feels proud to be a member of the human race, a race capable of producing such artistic splendour and beauty. You feel it is an honour to set foot in the shop where these artisans work and sell their precious wares. It is as if they are sharing a sacred mystery with you. You feel proud of all this labour and creativity and yet humbled at the same time. And thankful! The last time I felt a similar confluence of feeling was a good thirty years ago when I purchased a beautiful báinín jacket in Ó Máille's shop, in Galway. The sense of pride of the man in the shop who sold that jacket was palpable. So too was my own growing sense of Irishness and self-respect. Is there a lesson there somewhere? The sense of pride only lasted a short time, unfortunately, and within six months the poor báinín jacket was cast aside—it made me feel a bit like a tourist in my own country.

first light of day
the excitement
of green parrots

Urgent Announcement…On our way from Modinagal to Rishikesh. A prominent sign: "SPEAK ENGLISH FLUENTLY: PERSONALITY IMPROVEMENT". Now for you!

Rishikesh (the "Tresses of the Sages"). On the narrow streets of Rishikesh, the motorbikes swivel and swerve to avoid hitting the sacred cows. A pig ambles along the street also. It roots in the earth for a moment, then raises its head, aristocratically. Maybe the poor pig thinks she's a cow? Saints and sinners making their way through the crowds—it is never easy to discern between them. A simpleton greets me, a joyful smile on his face. Or maybe he is a great sage and I just don't know it? Nothing comes close to Rishikesh, nothing except Lourdes on LSD or Knock on cocaine. It is to this place and the ashram of Maharishi Mahesh Yogi that the Beatles came a long time ago. Day and night, the divine name (Ram) is on the edge of every beggar's lips. "Ram Ram, Jai! Ram!" An eternal litany.

An old woman sits at the head of a bridge and she has the look of someone who can commune only with God: "Ram, Ram, Jai! Ram!" Is this the expression of a devout nature or a repetitious parroting of words, I ask myself? If Ram! Ram! (the last words which Gandhi uttered prior to his assassination) are the passwords to Heaven, then this woman has already entered into the glory.

I spot a foreign couple on the bank of the Ganges taking part in the arthi, the ceremony of flames and flowers. Two Americans, dressed like Hindus. The man looks a bit uncomfortable and restless but the woman's face is lit up in a beatific smile. Are women more spiritual than men by nature? I wonder. Have they got a greater understanding of the life force, of life's very source itself?

A person dressed in white sits in meditative pose on a rock near the river. He has the look of a heron; the fish he seeks is his own soul. Despite the crowds and the clamour, this person—whoever he is—has carved out his own space for a period of silent contemplation. It could be, of course, that there is nothing of substance passing through his mind, just the murmur of the river. Maybe he's just seeking a refuge from life's burdens and responsibilities, many Westerners might say. But no, that isn't really the case here. In this country, meditation is part of everyday life; it is the food and drink of living and the man on the rock knows this very well. People have been visiting Rishikesh for a thousand years and more to find this out for themselves. And if, in the end, this world is nothing else but the flesh "Mealladh go mór iad ord na gCaipisíneach" (the Capuchins have been greatly deceived) as the old epigram goes.

Here the cow knows that she is blessed amongst animals, that the streets belong to her. That said, she never appears conceited or stuck-up. The opposite is the case, in fact. She epitomizes gentleness and humility. She has something royal about her, something of the matriarch. Unfortunately, one cannot help noticing that some of the cows here are suffering from diseases and ailments of various types. The majority of the people of India are so poor that they can often barely look after their own health, never mind that of their cattle.

I pass a group of children sitting in a hut. They are practicing their chanting in unison, venerating Krishna. It is obvious from their singing that they have already put in long hours of practice. Are their rights as children being infringed, I wonder? What about their right to play and have fun, their right to laughter? Who are they? Orphans? Why were they—and not others—chosen for this chanting work? Or is it the case that this is a form of play for them? Is this opportunity to chant the greatest gift any parent can bestow on their child or is an injustice being perpetrated on them? Only Krishna can tell.

Archaeologists can tell us what Clonmacnoise once looked like and what daily life was like at other holy sites throughout Ireland in centuries past. And yet do any of us really understand what is meant by Celtic spirituality? Can we really grasp that peculiar form of holiness and devotion that drove monks to the beehive huts on Skellig Michael; do we accept that miracles really occurred or do we view the hagiographic tradition as a collection of legends? The wonderful thing about ancient places such as Rishikesh and other ancient and more remote parts of the Himalayas, as described by Swami Rama for instance, is that little has changed here for thousands of years. If one sets aside the perspective of the tourist for a short moment and strikes out into the wilderness alone, one can sense the concerns of this world as encapsulated within something much greater and much wilder, something more Other. The familiar and the strange woven as one.

For this section of our trip we have joined an organised tour. Incredible as it may seem, there are two Irish people amongst this group, both of whom Eithne knows. Altogether, the group comprises six English people (our guide included), six Irish people and one American. Altogether it is noticeable that the Irish are sticking together as one group, the English likewise. The American seems to be a loner although he tells us that Jesus is watching over him. His two staples are his bottle of whiskey in one pocket and his copy of the Bible, in the other. The American's name is Tom and he is sharing a tent with another Tom—"Tom the Brit" whom we have re-named "Spiderman". This is a reference to the web of tattoos that covers his body. This morning Spiderman rose from his sleep with the mother of all hangovers. He drank half a bottle of whiskey last night—(Indian beer isn't great, so he stuck to the whiskey) and he says to me now in a wavering voice: "Is that car over there moving or is it just me?" As far as I can tell neither he nor the car is moving! I find out later that Spiderman isn't used to drinking whiskey at all—but that, after a blast of the Old Testament from the other Tom the previous evening—the extract where Noah and the ancients spent forty days and forty nights in the Ark—both of them lashed into the whiskey! May Jahweh bring salvation to both of them and lead them out of the Deluge.

Our group visits many temples and views many statues, the Hindus staring at Spiderman all the while. Well, as our guide back in Mumbai told us a

while back—isn't God present in the spider itself? Christ revealed himself to his own disciples as the King of Creation. Krishna did the same when in the presence of Arjuna; as Arjuna says in the Bhagavad-Gita, the Divine Poem:
"I see You without beginning, without middle, without end…" Where is India's beginning and where is its end? This is the question, of course. India's ruling party, the BJP (Bharatiya Janata Party) is trying to define India from a primarily Hindu perspective. India is a larger and more diverse country than this definition, however. Given the country's nuclear capability, it is important that the more extreme aspects of this nationalism are kept under a tight rein; otherwise Jumma, Kashmir and Assam could explode in a ball of fire and fury with winds of lamentation coming from the ruins of Pakistan, unless they strike first.

"What brought us here, anyway?" one of our travel group asks. "There is nothing here. And the beds are as hard as a rock." You make your bed and then you lie on it, I think to myself. Why would anybody go on a package holiday titled "Sailing Down the Eternal Ganges" complete with organised trips, if it was comfort that they were seeking? It is difficult to say. Of course, if you don't appreciate that the mantras intoned consistently here are holy words, then you would be forgiven for thinking that people here are just spouting a load of gibberish on a regular basis—the same gibberish, more or less, which British colonial forces once heard in Ireland.

It is not the cock crowing which wakes us at six o'clock in the morning here in Rishikesh but the sound of the mahamantra, the great Hare Krishna mantra which echoes beautifully throughout the town. I think of all our relatives and friends back home in Ireland who will wake soon to the sound of the alarm clock. Alarm, mind you! What a terrible way to begin a new day!

We visit another temple today, one that is in Uttarkashi in the Himalayas. (The word uttar has the same etymology as uachtar (cream/ uachtarach/upper) in Irish. This temple is smaller than many of the others and it honours Shiva. It has a fine linga, a Holy Penis, decorated with golden flowers. We all pay our humble respects to the Penis. Well, as they say: "When in Rome, do as the Romans do". The American is thirsty after the experience.

"Nach fada fairsing í Éire" ("Is not Ireland a big and spacious country?"), as Peig Sayers once said. What would Peig say if she was standing here now, the Himalayan peaks tipping the horizon, one mountain peak higher than the next. Small wonder so many saints, poets and wise men all gathered here. We are now at the roof of the world. The night is ours, so croon the cicadas, as the light cascade of their music emerges from every bush and tree. Lights appear here and there in the foothills. It is only here in the holy mountains and the expansive glens of the Himalayas that one can truly appreciate the iconology of light and fire. Only here can one truly understand why they have an almost sacramental significance. Just a few generations ago the prayer "Nár mhúcha Dia solas na bhFlaitheas orainn" (May God never quench his Heavenly Light on us") was uttered in Ireland as the night-candle was put out. The flick of a switch changed all of that; light lost all of its magic. The sun and the moon no longer generate the same respect or awe as they once did, in the Western world at least. Who today would write lines similar to von Eichendorff's

Es schienen so golden die Sterne
Am Fenster ich einsam stand…
(How golden shine the stars as I stand alone by the window).

Rather than look at the sun, the moon and the stars what do we Westerners do today? We watch the weather forecast on the television. If the sun shines and we are unaware of its glory, what meaning is there in such a phrase as, "Is tú grian m'anama" –(You are the sun of my soul)? The meaning of 'sun-worship' has changed somewhat over time.

May the sun light our way today, tomorrow and forever. Amen. That is my prayer as I stand here in the Himalyas.

There is a problem with the hot water in the Sivalinga Hotel, where we are stay tonight. We have to buy a bucket of hot water—ten rupees a bucket and throw it over ourselves; think of it as a ritual. I imagine the American washing himself in another room and being reborn!

We are on our way to Gangotri, originally the traditional source for the

Ganges—(the glacier moved since then). The road is so rough here that if somebody were to open my notebook now they would think I was writing in Sanskrit and not Irish. An rud a scríobhann an púca … (Whatever the pooka writes the pooka can read, as they say…)

In a Holy Cave…In Gangotri, there is a cave dedicated to the legendary saint Sai Baba whose image is found all over India. I make my way into the cave where the local baba has lit a fire. Om Sai Baba, Hari Om he intones continually to himself and to the fire, in soft maternal tones. He prepares a chapatti for me in the ashes and I eat it slowly. This food is known as prasad, blessed food, an offering, a sacrament. In this small smoke-filled cave, I feel the sacredness of India more intensely than I did in any temple before this. The baba has been in this cave twenty years and he couldn't care less whether it's ten rupees I leave him or one hundred. His concerns are not of this world. Om Sai Baba, Hari Om!

a dead cow:
the silence of the Himalayas
cackling vultures

We've travelled nine kilometres today by mule, as far as Chid-Basa. You won't find this place on any map. This is a tea-and-biscuit station complete with the Indian cigarette brand known as Wills, a brand nobody smokes. Most ordinary Indians smoke the bidi, a rough home-made cigarette. (The incomparable sage Sri Nisargadatta Maharaj was a bidi seller).

The air is thin here; we are so high up that if my mule were to slip even slightly it would be curtains. We would fall right over the edge. Our guide keeps the mule on the straight and narrow, however. He talks to the animal continually, encourages it along every step of the journey. He speaks to the mule in its own language, cajoling and warning it when necessary. The mule plods on at a steady pace. The muleteer has no English and from time to time I try to work out whether he is talking to me or issuing an instruction to the mule. Around certain corners, there are low-hanging branches and he warns me to lower my head. I look around behind me…where is Eithne? The muleteer gives a rough shout—“Don’t turn around!” is what I take it to mean. Another shout—“Don’t look down”, is it? Holy macaroni, what is he saying at all? The mule lets off a fart…a volley that resonates across the mountains. “Let me down,” I say to the muleteer.

I need to take a break. Eithne and the others have gone ahead to see the glacier. I’m happy enough to imagine what it looks like—or look at a photo of it sometime in the future. I spend a few minutes sitting under a tree, a few minutes of contemplation. The chirping of an odd bird the only sound. It is in a place like this that you really understand what brought the monks to Glendalough and to Sceilg Mhichíl (Skellig Michael). You couldn’t but contemplate the Alpha and the Omega in this place, the Beginning and the End, ultima rerum. The crow here gives out a hoarse croak. Soon it’ll be completely silent. The gigantic mountains demand silence here. The unfathomable silence of infinity. The crowns of the Himalayas beneath their perpetual snow-caps; their crowns will never disappear, it doesn’t matter what humanity endures between now and the Last Day. Come along warmongers, try out your weapons against the might of the Himalayas.

the sun over the Himalayas –
my mule
drinks from the Ganges

The muleteers are smoking ganja. (Ganga is the river while ganja is the drug; both are godlike, according to the legend). I have named my mule Foinavon in memory of that ghostly horse that won the Grand National years ago. Pat Taaffe was in the saddle and Micheál O'Hehir was the only race commentator to recognise him as he emerged from the fog.

It is time to get on the move again. I didn't see much of the glacier. Foinavon, long-eared and long-suffering; be clear and sure-footed on our way back to Gangotri, will you? And if you happen to get thirsty, always remember that the Ganges is one hundred feet below us. Good on you Mumbai-woman. If you were here now, would you say that there is a god in this mule? If there is—and I don't deny it—please don't let me down now. You couldn't die in a more blessed place, that is for sure…but still and all.

One of the group tells us a story about a trip he took to Egypt and a donkey who fell over the edge of a cliff. He did not slip or fall asleep, this donkey. No…he did it deliberately! The donkey was an unbeliever, overcome by a fit of despair. And here's me hoping that the mules of the Himalayas have a more robust faith than their Egyptian counterparts and wouldn't dream of giving up the ghost—by putting a hoof in the wrong place.

The tea-sellers stare at us as we leave them behind. Maybe they are jealous? Maybe they are sore with us about something? Their faces are inscrutable and it is impossible to know what they are thinking. Those same tea-sellers will soon gather their things together and journey southwards. A few sadhus will remain behind, hermits for whom the predicted snowfalls hold no fear.

Praise be the King of Mules… It's the same endurance test on the narrow trail back. Have I ever travelled eighteen kilometres like this before? If so, it wasn't in this life. The muleteers are leading the mules as they do; the rest of us are praying!

I am given an abrupt instruction—in sign language—to keep a tight hold on the back of the saddle any time we pass through a rocky hollow—Foinavon picking her way through carefully. Hopefully you've been here before in a previous life, I whisper to the poor mule. On she moves, immune to the belts of the muleteer as we negotiate the most treacherous and narrowest of corners. I know when we have reached the most dangerous spots because the muleteer speaks to the mule in a soft tone, somewhat like the Irish call to goats—"suc, suc" - and then louder again "roits! roits!", whatever that means in the language of mules.

Gangotri! I can see it below me now, a long way below. Yes…it definitely is Gangotri. I recognise the Post Office—the place where they ran out of stamps yesterday. And over there is the temple! We are safe again!

It was four o'clock in the afternoon by then and the first job is to buy a bucket of warm water and to have a wash. We will seek out a quiet spot and find something to eat; the place we went to last night was so noisy you could hardly hear yourself think; an electric generator sounding out through the night.

Passing through the town of Tehri…One thing is certain. We will never see this place again, no matter how long we live. An enormous dam is being built here with the help of the Russians. The work has been going on for years. Sometime in the near future, this entire area will be covered in water. The building of dams is the source of much controversy in India with many writers opposed to these developments (including Arundhati Roy, the author of The God of Small Things, a book Eithne is reading at the moment). Other writers have remained silent. If there was an earthquake in a place like this, what would happen? The authorities maintain that everything is well-built and everybody would be safe. But then they say the same thing about the nuclear stations. Everybody will be fine, everybody will be safe! I spot a monkey on the roof of a house. Will he be told when it's time for him to cash in his chips and move on?

a rotten banana
thrown on a rubbish heap
a mule devours it

We are in Dayopriyag, the Place of the Gods—what else would it be called! The Meeting of the Waters, the Bhagirathi and the Alaknanda. A confluence of the worldly and the heavenly. There is a delay on the journey, the road blocked because of a landslide. Men with explosives are out on the road to blow away the debris. It is more of a track than a road to be honest; it is so narrow that a cow could barely pass another, and I think of the origin of the Irish word for a road, a cow passing another cow, bó thar bhó, bóthar. Once through, we have a long journey ahead. Eighteen hours of travelling to reach Allahabad on the banks of the Yamuna, the place where the great Mela is held, the biggest gathering of pilgrims in the world.

I had half-vowed not to taste any Indian beer but I give in to the temptation when the American offers me a bottle after we board the train. I don't drink it, however. It is the hordes of poor beggars, children for the most part, who get to taste my beer. They are so poor here that they crowd around any stranger who might be able to give them something to eat or drink. It is chaos in the train station, the Seven Battalions of the Fianna wouldn't be able to keep order on the people that swarm around here.

In the station the arrival and departure of the trains is everybody's point of focus. There is a dog trapped between the railings of the train; his head is stuck between the metal bars but nobody takes the slightest notice of him. The American is writing something down in his notebook. Three lines. Could it be a haiku? I don't like to be nosy… in the end I find out that it is an account of what he has eaten today. If he should get terribly sick from food poisoning at least his doctor will know what antidote to prescribe. He's taking care of his health! Of course, if he were to fall very sick, he wouldn't be able to drink alcohol either, I suppose. The American cuts the bottom out of a plastic bottle with a scissors and uses the new container as a drinking glass of sorts. Necessity is the mother of invention. We discuss American poetry. Did I know Allen Ginsberg's work? I tell the American that I actually met Ginsberg once, in Dublin. He appeared in Bewley's café one day, at the same time as a new book of poems was being launched by Michael Davitt. Our chat stirs some recollections of the old days, the days of the poetry journal INNTI and I realise how much I miss the literary camaraderie of those heady days. The zest for argument. The bitching that went on; the imagination stirring in unexpected ways, the malice, and the put-down, and all the visionary aspects of that whole enterprise. That was a period of our lives when we all seemed to have certain goals to aim for. Those powerful currents and eddies have faded now. I can barely recall that communal river flowing or any of its diverse inspirational currents which once energized us all. Time to revisit the Sixties?

Poetry is a not just a hobby. It is a necessity, as Rilke says in his Letters to a Young Poet. If the inner compulsion isn't there, forget it.

"Did you say something, just there?" the bearded American asks.

"No, nothing," I respond. "I was just muttering to myself." He prises the lid from the top of the bottle and takes a peek out through the curtains of the train compartment, checks to see if there any porters about. I take a good slug of this stuff which passes for Scotch. If it was half monkey-piss, that wouldn't surprise me one bit. (Is the rumour true that I drank urine once on a Cork stage while playing a bit-part in a play written by Seán Ó Tuama? Unfortunately, it is indeed true. My line was, 'Mún eilifint breoite'—'the piss of a sick elephant' and, indeed, the jug I drank from contained that substance . Human urine. How was it? The play or the urine? Neither was particularly good, to tell you the truth).

"Who's with you in this carriage?" I ask the American. Normally you have to book a compartment with sleeping facilities in advance. "Haven't a clue," he says. "Spiderman is on his own tonight…by all accounts." In the morning I find out that he got no chance to drink during the night as he had the ticket collector sharing the carriage with him.

A Hindu family are in the same sleeping compartment as Eithne and myself. A man, a woman and their daughter. I couldn't help but note the diligence with which the daughter was looking after her father—and he wasn't that elderly, really. She gets him his pills and makes sure he is properly covered with a blanket. He shapes himself beneath the blanket, his legs bundled under him like a yogi.

I leave the light on for another small while and read about Mummidivaram Yogi (1930-1985) who was also known as the Bali Yogi. He spent most of his life sitting in the same position, without eating or drinking. He spent forty years sitting in the same place and not a crumb passed his lips. Would you believe that? I've heard even stranger stories than this; I'll tell them again sometime.

We make camp on a sand-bank, along the edge of the Ganges. The boatmen erect the tents for us and make another small camp which can function as a toilet—a big hole in the sand and a wooden board laid over it. You'd have to be a real yogi to do your business here. A small group of locals come over to have a look at us. It seems that we are the focus of a good number of jokes. They stare at us and have a good laugh. You can't blame them; if we were to see ourselves through their eyes I'm sure we too would think ourselves a bunch of ragamuffins.

The sun has gone down but a lingering residue of pink light still hangs over the Ganges—she's like a bride on her honeymoon night. A bird cries out from the opposite bank of the river. An egret, possibly. There are 108 different names for the Ganges but the most beautiful of all is Ma, meaning "mother". I think of a tune and begin to chant out loud. "Ma Ma Ganga Ma, Ganga Ma Ganga Ma, Ma Ma Ganga Ma…"

There are small holes in the sand all around here. They are caused by gerbils somebody tells us. Who knows. The moon shines alone in the night sky. She lights up the dark with her benevolent smile. I bow to her.

The bright light of day. I'm no detective but it seems to me that something was wandering around the camp during the night. Was it a human being? An animal? Or was it the body of some dead person who heard my chanting and emerged from the Ganges seeking company? It was none of these things. It was the American, drunk as a lord! Some mad impulse came over him and he began wandering around in the black night outside. Spiderman had to go out and find him and drag him back to the camp. The blind leading the blind.

Somebody is washing himself in the Ganges. A man who has never heard the word "neurosis"—in any language—and who wouldn't understand the meaning of the word, even if it was explained to him. The bright waters of the Ganges; these same waters will carry away this man's ashes someday, man and river whispering their way towards eternity, freedom, or towards rebirth.

The boatmen are a surly and taciturn bunch. You'd know by them that they belong to a caste or a class all of their own. They speak to us just once during the course of our journey when they utter the word "dolphin" in their own language. "Sur! Sur!" River dolphins can be spotted here from time to time; they are said to be as blind as a bat. The American didn't see them as he was out for the count, stretched out in the back of the boat, flies dancing on him. Eithne is worried that the sun will burn him badly and she takes a hold of her newly-purchased scarf and places it over his face as a curtain.

We travel down the Ganges, the cook's boat accompanying us. Given the reputation India has for good tea, isn't it strange that we've drunk the most awful cups of tea on this trip so far—it's not tea as we know it but a milky, sweet chai from a kettle. The malaria pills we have to take are known as doxycycline. The American says that these ones are the best ones you can take and that they don't damage the kidneys or cause nightmares; better again, they are said to kill off the micro-organisms that cause food poisoning. Tom the American is probably right about that. We haven't been sick yet, praise be Ganga Ma. "Don't take these pills in the morning," Tom warns; the afternoon is the best time because they don't go well with the hot sun. Above all, don't take them with Rennies or any other chemical which aids indigestion. The American is a guru when it comes to pharmaceuticals by all accounts. He also advises us to avoid all perfumes and after-shaves because they only attract the mosquitoes.

The captain of our boat is smoking ganja at his leisure. He pulls noisily on an unusually-shaped pipe. The other day I was reading about a man who was addicted to ganja and beer, so much so that he wasn't getting any "buzz" from them any more. To increase his "buzz", he began to eat those reptiles you see on the walls here, those gecko-type creatures which have an incredibly strong poison in their bodies. At one point this man was eating four of these reptiles a day to get some kind of a "kick" from the juices. Not unnaturally, the experts are concerned about his health.

Our next stop is Varanasi, also known as Banares—or Kashi, the City of Light. It is here that the devout widows of India come to die. Well, it's better to hang around Varanasi waiting for death than to follow the older tradition of sati—the woman throwing herself on the burning corpse of her husband. We have to give the British some credit for that much, I suppose; it was they who outlawed the tradition of sati in 1829.

Under a full moon one of the boat-men is exercising on the banks of the Ganges. He's been rowing from early morning and there's not a pick on him. Pure muscle and sinew. It is strange to be in this place without the "staples" of civilization—newspapers, sports pages, radio, television, telephones, electricity—all of those other things which we take for granted back home—tea, toast, chocolate, washing-up liquid—and all the rest. All the "usual" sounds which we do not here in this place—the voices, the faces we don't see.

a corpse in the Ganges
a crow
takes a ride

Mantle of Blue …the slow throb of the oars is a new sound to my ears. Steady and rhythmic, the boatmen have been rowing from early morning until now—it is late evening. I am under a spell and have lost all sense of time and space—how far are we now from the opposite bank of the great river? Are we even within a scread asail (donkey's bray) of our destination? (Indians use the word "gaukos" to describe the distance travelled by a cow's lowing).

Sometimes the Ganges and the sky become one; water and sky knitted together in one great mantle of blue. I try to focus on what is happening near me. I look over in the direction of Krishna, the youngest of the boat-men. His eyes have a piercing quality; they are feral almost—as if they could see right through you—the eyes of a leopard. They are eyes that pierce the soul, eyes which say: "I do not recognise you—I am not of your kind."

Var-an-asi, Var-an-asi, the oars whisper over and over in a mantra of their own.

I have a chat with the two eldest bar-men in the Hindusthan Hotel. They are Bengalis and one of them goes by the name of Kali Prasad Bhattacharya. He enjoys the fact that I can work out the etymology of both his forename and his surname. Kali, the goddess of destruction, a goddess who sports a dozen shells around her neck, whose tongue protrudes from her mouth. It isn't everybody—every Hindu even— who understands what these skulls stand for—death of the ego. I'm not going to approach this subject at this stage, however. Prasad means holy food; it is a sweet food usually, a food that is distributed at the puja ceremony. And I think that the suffix "-acharya" means "teacher". He is happy that I am correct about this etymology. The other barman is Amitava Guha; Amitava is actually another name for the Buddha, the Light that is never Extinguished.

About 50% of the people in Varanasi are of Bengali origin, Kali informs me. This region was even once referred to as the "Second Bengal". "50%?" says Amitava, and a frown comes over his face. "It's only about 40%", he says. It would appear, initially at least, that the two colleagues are in disagreement. But this doesn't actually prove to be the case. Amitava's shake of the head actually indicates that he is agreeing with Kali. It takes a while to become familiar with the cultural nuances of India. Next moment, the two men agree to split the difference as regards how many Bengalis there are in Varanasi. The discussion assumes the status of a negotiation—they are like two dealers trying to agree on an acceptable price. In the end both men agree that the percentage of Bengalis in Varanasi is about 15% - a figure which is a good deal lower than the original estimates.

"I wouldn't be too sure about that figure either," says Kali, when he sees me scribbling the figure 15% in my notebook. "There isn't any real certainty about the accuracy of that figure," he says solemnly—as if we were now considering one of the most important subjects in the world. More important even than how many thousands of soldiers are now currently stationed in Kashmir, say. This latter subject is an issue that is so sensitive, it can't even be discussed in a public bar. The military might of India; men between the ages of 15 and 49 years of age: 164,410,462.

Let's consider religious and philosophical issues for a moment. Kali visited Goa once, he tells me, Goa which was once a Portuguese colony but is now part of India. It wasn't only the British who were in India. The French spent some time in Pondicherry and the Germans and the Danish tried to get their slice of the big pie too. Moving on…although, Kali is a devout Hindu—with a name like Kali, he'd have to be—he was curious about other religions at one point in his life. One of his friends brought him to Mass one Sunday where he received Holy Communion. I didn't tell Kali that the priest is normally not meant to offer Holy Communion to a non-believer—something told me that Kali was very much a believer in God anyway. He seemed to be accepting of every religion. Whatever the priest said as part of his sermon on that particular Sunday anyway, it annoyed Kali, and he never went back into a church again. Apparently the priest said something to the effect that all the gangsters in the films had Christian names—names such as John, Joe, Luigi etc.—and that this was a scandal. I was very surprised by this comment. To be honest, I don't think I really understand it—even now—what point the priest was making.

"Do you think that the Ganges is a goddess?" I ask Amitava and he looks out to peer intently at the river for a moment.

"Well," says he, "I wouldn't drink any of the water that's in the Ganges and I wouldn't bathe in it either." (This is a modern-thinking man that I have here, I say to myself).

"Who knows how many types of coli are in the Ganges. The river must be replete with them! And yet many thousands of people wash themselves in the Ganges every day and do not fall sick; their immune systems seem to get stronger, if anything. There is scientific evidence to support this. It is religious belief which overpowers all of the bugs and infections, the strength of the people's faith,"

"Mmm…" I mutter to myself. He hasn't really answered my question at all!

a ghat in Varanasi
a woman's leg
not yet licked by flames

"From a religious point of view, what are the biggest differences between you and us?" I ask him.

"There is no difference between us," Amitava responds. "We are all human beings." He stares into my eyes as he gives his response, searching for my reaction. And I don't contradict him. Kali adds his tuppence worth then. The biggest difference he thinks is that Westerners are always eager to increase their material wealth while the Indian searches for peace of mind.

"Really?" I am unsure now about some of these propositions but Kali backs up his assertion with a blast from the Old Sanskrit: Rajadhana, gadjadhana, bahridhana aur santoshdhana—saba dhana dhuri saman …

"Right," I say.

"What I've just listed there is an inventory of all the different types of wealth one can accumulate—land or jewels or livestock—all of them are worthless to the person who is without peace of mind."

"Ok," I say and we have to bring the conversation to an end there and then. "My train is leaving shortly". I leave a tip on the table behind me.

The journey back to Delhi is seven hundred miles; more than enough time to consider this conversation as relating to the meaning of life. On the streets of Varanasi I see cripples who have neither the material comfort of a home nor any peace of mind; they crawl along the best they can, their stumps of limbs exposed. They have neither fingers nor toes. An Indian man accosts me in that space between the train carriages where the people go to smoke, to clean their mouths or even their tongues. The door separating the train compartments is often kept open here; it is a door which provides a beautiful window on the Indian countryside. He is interested in temperature statistics. I give him some food for thought (I think) when I tell him that the temperature rarely falls below freezing point in Ireland. Nobody in Ireland remembers the Night of the Big Snow anymore, never mind the Night of the Big Wind.

"We have a temperate climate in Ireland," I tell my Indian friend. Here in India it is just 6.30 am in the morning and it is already very hot. Can he have my address, the man asks?

"Certainly, you're most welcome to it," I respond. The man tells me that he is looking forward to our future correspondence by post—a correspondence confined to the subject of temperatures.

"You cool," he tells me. Does this comment refer to my body temperature? I'm really looking forward to receiving his first letter.

Monkey in a Poke… I take a photo of a small monkey. It is a wearing a red dress and is dancing a reel. A youth runs up behind me—"500 rupees", he calls out.

"Eh?"

"Five hundred rupees. He's my monkey. He's my business! Monkey…dance…photograph.

"I'm not interested in buying the monkey!" I say.

"Buy monkey? Five hundred rupees?!"

"No. I don't…" I hand the man a hundred rupees and leave as fast as my legs can carry me.

Noam Chomsky gives a lecture in Delhi on the 5th of September, where he says:

"There is a growing realisation that in the present system, capital is a priority and people are incidental." I like the phrase "the present system"; at least another system is possible. Professor Chomsky is termed an anti-American. This isn't an accurate description of the man, however. He is a patriot in my view, a real and true American. What drives him is the belief that his fellow-Americans are overly-fixated on materialism, a materialism which blinds people to the exploitation carried out in their name.

One of the people who attends the poetry reading in the Academy greets me courteously afterwards. "I am Nirankar Narain Saxena. I write teras!"

"Fair play to you", I reply, and I am racking my brains to think what the devil the term teras means? It's not a term which I can recall coming across in the Princeton Handbook of Multicultural Poetries in anywhere else for that matter. It's better to be honest with him.

"I am not sure what these teras of yours are, I'm afraid." He doesn't class me as an ignoramus, thankfully. It is the opposite, in fact. He is delighted that my intellectual curiosity is still burning; that I have the humility to continually augment my limited store of human knowledge.

"How could you have heard of them, my friend? Nobody knows what teras are!" I feel a hundred times better already...well…not exactly. "It's a new form of writing. I created it! Myself!"

"Good for you," I say, congratulating him. "Would…would you have a sample of your work with you at all?" He sure does. He reaches into his pocket and hands me a book.

"I'd like to buy your book!"

"No, it's yours. You have it!" he says.

"This new form is a verse of thirteen words. They are not hiku," he says.

"Hiku? You mean haiku, is it?"

"Yes, they are not hiku…they are called teras!"

I begin to read and my eyes widen with surprise. I have only read two lines; is this for real? I re-read those two lines once more. Am I reading them correctly? Yes I am. These teras are…how shall I put it?

"150 rupees," the poet blurts out suddenly. I am taken by surprise. I thought it was a gift?

"Would you have change of a 500 rupee note?" He stares down at the note in my hand and I can tell by the look on the man's face that he is not happy; it's unlikely that he'll be able to break the 500 rupee note. He ransacks his purse and his pockets and then hands me a small bunch of notes. I don't bother to count them. After all, what price can anyone put on a teras? I read the biographical note on the back of the book. It says that the man is a bachelor and he lives an extremely busy life. This isn't a non-sequitur. There is definitely some link between these various facts of his existence.

"Will you sign it for me?" A beaming smile lights up his face. I get the feeling that today is a special day for this teras writer, a day similar say to one's first visit to the zoo. He signs the book for me: "With love".

Jaysus, I've just met him and he already loves me. I better read one of the poems.

"Ah…you picked the best one", he says. Here it is:

Pray
Read write
Enjoy
If you please
Send comments
Yours truly, NN Saxena

He gives me a look. It's the look of a wandering spirit. He is a stray soul wandering at dawn; a soul who harbours many hopes and dreams, one of which is the following: Maybe this visiting poet can provide him with sustenance from this day forward? I'm not sure whether to laugh or to cry. Says I to myself: "Your work will be read even when Kalidasa, Bihari and Tagore have been forgotten—but not until then!" He is still staring at me intently.

"Why..?" I say. I'm trying to think of something to say.

"Sorry?"

"Yes, why…? Why thirteen words?"

His old smile is back again. He is about to share one of the biggest mysteries of the East with me.

"Isn't thirteen an unlucky number?"

"Hmm, I believe so, Mr Saxena."

"The teras will refute that long-held theory," says Nirankar Narain Saxena M.A.

I buy Malgudi Days, a collection of simply-written short stories by the writer R.K. Narayan. I don't bother checking the price. "One eighty rupees", the woman in the shop says. I give her 180 rupees. What I haven't understood, of course, is that "One 80 rupees" is what she was actually saying. Eighty rupees was the real price of that book. Earlier, the taxi driver played the same trick on us "One fifty rupees", he said, when the prices was actually 50. I handed him 150 rupees. Will I ever learn?

morning turns to marble
bright echoing of doves
Taj Mahal

We see a collection of green-coloured plates in the Taj Museum, plates noted for the fact that they once changed colour on contact with poisoned food. The museum officials and tour guides are yawning with tiredness. It occurs to me that a live experiment for the tourists including poison plates would attract a much bigger crowd of visitors to the museum. After seeing everything there is to see in the Taj, we are brought to a workshop where descendants of the men who built the Taj are still working with white marble. Hunched over their tools, they demonstrate their skills and it is as if nothing has changed in a thousand years. They are still slaving away the same as their ancestors before them. These artisans are Moslems and yet they do not object to carving small statuettes of the Buddha. The Taliban, destroyers of Buddhist statues, wouldn't be too happy with this.

I really enjoy Malgudi Days and I make a mental note to read some of Narayan's novels when I get the chance. There is a line in one of the short stories that grabs my attention. It refers to the colonial era and it is an announcement on a train carriage which stated that there was room enough for 4 troops of British soldiers in one particular train carriage - or 6 troops of Indian soldiers!

We arrive at Agra train station at night, where we wait for the train to Delhi. The station is a cacophony of sounds; the shrill hammering of workmen undertaking repairs; the public announcements in Hindi (and then in English) which track the arrival and departure of the trains. The cries of the fruit-vendors and the tea-sellers who shout out their wares—chai, banana, nuts. It is one enormous tapestry of sound; each voice its own colour, its own unique aspect. Suddenly, the station goes quiet. What is it? A huge intake of breath? The noise resumes as quickly as it came to a stop. I hear chanting from a local temples, there is the whirr of a mosquito in my ear. Three-wheeled taxis sound their horns; as if heralding the Day of Judgement. A woman snores innocently close to us; the cleaners work their brushes along the floor; somebody gives a three-legged dog a kick; the cry of an abandoned dog. The sound of the train-whistle; the screech of train upon train. Is it any wonder Buddha journeyed to India and preached a philosophy of silence.

Farewell to India…Our last night in India is spent in the company of Shantosh and Rama, two women of note. Shantosh has climbed Mount Everest twice; she's the only woman to have done so. Shantosh is both humble and ambitious in equal measure. She would love to see change in India. She's not alone there. And Rama? She's a female version of Micheál Mac Liammóir, you could say. No sign of her in the Guinness Book of Records yet, but it is only a matter of time. They'll assign to her a new category in the book. Rama's graceful hands are covered in henna and there is something dramatic and true about the way she turns her head and listens; as we made conversation. This is a woman who would not understand small-talk—the like of "Isn't it a lovely day today!" She wouldn't put up with chatter like that; no, she would be angry, angry and heartbroken. Why waste the precious gifts you have been given on such idle gossip? Already, she is hoping to come to Ireland as part of a troop of female Indian artists. What can we do to help? Maybe there is an Arts Festival in Kiltemagh or somewhere that would welcome an Indian theme for their festival? Maybe Shantosh could climb Croke Patrick? I am more than happy to invite a troop of female artists to Ireland but where would we put them? Out house has only four bedrooms and anyway—what form of art do these people practice? How many people is a troop? Ten? Twenty people? What do they meant by a visit? A week? A month? Are they dancers? Rama is speaking; she is explaining something; she is in mid-sentence—it's a long sentence; she replies to our questions with her hands. I think they must be dancers…or circus performers? Difficult to tell.

Rama brings us to the Russian Cultural Centre in Delhi, a place where poets gather to recite their verse! I am asked to read a few poems in Irish and English and the rest of the night passes through the medium of Hindi. Rama sits next to me and translates some verses here and there. The night is beautiful, poetry cascading like stained glass! I know this is a strange metaphor to employ…but this is a strange night. One man reads his poetry in Urdu, a language with a long literary pedigree and with which any self-respecting Indian writer is familiar. This is not the reserved and stuffy gathering of many modern-day poetry festivals in the West. No, here the poets shout out their praises to each of their fellow-poets in turn; they sing out their praises, with gusto and pride.

Wah! Wah! Wah!…they shout out and it is similar to a sean-nós session back in Ireland—the audience calling out their admiration, their respect, "Mo ghrá do sciúch!" (Bless you voice!) or "Dia go Deo Leat!" (God be with you!

forever!) Public poetry? No. Contemporary classical poetry is what this is.

Afterwards, we head for the Press-Club of India to wet the whistle. Preparations are being put in place for the great festival of Diwali. The roads were packed with giant trucks, making their four-day (and night) journey between here and Mumbai. In a month's time the Sikhs will hold their festival; a month later, it will be Christmas. Rama tells us that the Hindu fundamentalists are objecting to the celebration of Christmas. They consider the Christmas spirit to be nothing more than the decadent influence of the West, of television. The Christians here do not celebrate Diwali; why should Moslems celebrate Christmas? I thank Rama for introducing the poets at this gathering. I have been lucky enough to come into contact with a group of poets who are not happy to celebrate or suffer alone; or drown themselves as so many Swiss poets have done in recent years. Instead, they drown themselves in sound. Wah! Wah! Wah! they exclaimed throughout the evening; striking the table loudly to show approval of an image, a thought, a rhythm, words and feelings shared as communal food. Everybody at the gathering is included; each person shares in drinks or the toast. In this place there is still a respect for the reverence for the word, for the music of life. The poetic impetus is held in high regard. So too the nature of the words, the questioning mind , the troubled heart, eternal longing, doubt, despair, courage and self-reflection, the tangled confusion of life. Here is a poem written by Professor Satchidanandan:

Rip Van Winkle
Twenty years asleep
And it is still the same,
I'm going back to sleep
Wake me when something changes.
And I will tell you how this
life was once.
I will describe it so
You too will long to return.

Kowloon...gazing at the night skyline of the city of Hong Kong. The rainbow of water flowing slowly. Strange and exotic foods are on offer in the restaurants here—deer's penis amongst them. We meet a group of Australians in the hotel. Australians are well able to wet their beaks I can tell you. We were out of practice. I remember very little about Hong Kong to be honest. I hope we had a good time there; that is all I can say about it at this point.

Swords prohibited …The Sakura Hotel (called after the cherry blossoms) is the cheapest hotel in Tokyo. We read through the hotel's book of rules; it's like a phone directory it's so big, the regulations written in a style that is as bare as it is direct. You are instructed to wear the yukata every night—especially if you venture down the passage to have a shower in one of the communal areas. The yukata is like a long dress. It gives me the appearance of a samurai. You are not allowed to bring a sword into the hotel premises either. A reasonable-enough regulation, if you ask me. We have received an invitation from an avant-garde haiku publisher to attend an event where a number of haiku-related publications are being celebrated in unison. Everybody is bowing and genuflecting to one another like we are all emperors. My renku-master—(renku is a form of linked verse which gave birth to the haiku) Professor 'Shinku' Fukuda and a fellow member of an international renku group, Fusako Matano, accompany us to the event. (I am a member of the Milky Way Renku Society, as it happens). The event involves three-and-half hours of long speeches and short haiku readings, all in Japanese. Our minds are like jelly by the end of it, we are so tired. I am then asked to read a couple of haiku in both Irish and Japanese, a request which I duly fulfil with a translator.

The food at the break (half-time) is beautiful. Yes, this is as intense as a haiku Semi-Final—except for the fact that I am unable to read the score.

The gathering remains incredibly polite and patient for the entire duration of the event—until it is time to go home, that is. Then they bolt out of there in such a mad rush that you'd swear they had seen the figure of Murchadh na nDóiteán himself, or the Japanese equivalent of the notorious Earl of Inchiquin. The organiser of this event was a man by the name of Ban'ya Natsuishi and from what I could gather, everybody was there to sing his praises. There are actually thousands of haiku societies and clubs in Japan and they cooperate or compete with one another in equal measure. Poor Ban'ya has a lot of rivals, apparently. Like him, his wife is also a haiku poet. "Ní neart go cur le chéile," as we say in Irish. (Unity is strength).

We return to the hotel by underground train. On each platform there are barricades which open only when the train has come to a complete stop—this is to prevent people committing suicide apparently. I read the hotel regulations again. You are not permitted to enter the hotel if you are drunk or if you are suffering from an infectious disease. Instructions are given on what to do if there is an earthquake. I'm too whacked to read any further. It's time to hit the sack. A pair of bunkbeds.

The coffee the next morning is badly needed. We can't order any toast—if they have toast for breakfast—because we have very little Japanese (mostly haiku and renku related). We keep an eye on the other tables; what are the others ordering? Just coffee so far. Where is my book of useful phrases when you need it? Ah! Here is my small dictionary of words and phrases. Kondomu—(condom)—No. That's not what I need. Hanarero. "Get lost"—no, that's not what I need either. If I had to memorize every phrase on this one page alone in the phrasebook , I'd go get dizzy. I might get knocked down by a bus and instead of asking for a doctor—isha o yonde kudasai I might say something ridiculous like: "A condom please, no sugar and a hototogisu, (a cuckoo… he makes his appearance in millions of haiku). That wouldn't do, at all, at all.

Tokyo has 100,000 restaurants, believe it or not, and the one that we've found seems to serve coffee only. I resort to sign language and make strange noises with my mouth—"toast-a", "toast-u" etc. Hurrah! The waitress understands me. OK, it's toast that we get instead of whale's willy or whatever. I shouldn't be joking about these things, really. Food is an element in the vocabulary of racism, after all. When we told some Indian people that we intended visiting Japan, they were horrified—the Japanese eat the naga they said—the holy snake.

Just around the corner is the Salvation Army, the best army ever to come out of Britain. They appear to be well-funded.

Behind times … a toilet with a button which heats up the seat. Only an idle person could invent a device as strange as that. We feel a certain freedom here—relief might be a better word—relief from the craziness of India. I'll never forget the chaos of traffic that was Rishikesh; inside the cab of a three-wheeled taxi I glanced across towards another taxi that had pulled in alongside us. "Do you need a taxi, babu?" asked the cab-driver opposite me. Janey Mac…can you not see that I'm in a taxi?!

Here in Tokyo I can't help noticing a black van spewing raucous propaganda. The racket! You'd think they were slaughtering chickens. These are the so-called uyoku, right-wing groups. Up with the Emperor! Down with the Barbarian! That sort of thing. The Princess is expecting a baby. Everybody is very happy for her, the uyoku, naturally—and ourselves, the Barbarians.

We get lost a couple of times in the giant railway station of Shinjuku through which 4,000,000 souls pass every day, including children off to extra classes at three o'clock in the morning. Poor things.

A man sitting across from us is fast asleep, his mouth agape. He wakes with a start. Checks his phone for messages. Nothing new within the last few minutes. He goes back to sleep for another short spell. I take a glance at a magazine that is close by. A young Japanese couple on the front cover photo. They are jogging along while a taller man runs behinds them. The tall man is wearing an American baseball cap. LEARN ENGLISH WHILE YOU RUN the caption reads. Is it time for Foras na Gaeilge to employ a few similar marketing techniques in relation to the Irish language? LEARN IRISH WHILE YOU SHOWER? Yes, if we can associate the genitive case with pleasurable feelings we will have made a fresh start.

We are keen to find out what is going in the world—see a news bulletin somewhere. I slot 100 yen into the television set but all I get for my trouble is a couple of wrestlers in an unholy embrace.

Tokyo is a mixture of the ancient and the modern. I spot a comb-maker whose business is probably in the exact same place as it was during 15 generations of his people before him who have been comb makers. The combs are made from boxwood. How long more will this tradition last, however? The aping of Western values in Asia is a powerful force. Of course, the Western world does likewise and searches for aspects of Eastern life and culture; presumably both worlds will never become as one. It occurs to me that you could spend your whole life living in another country and yet you still wouldn't really understand half of the story. Is treise dúchas ná oiliúint, as we say in Irish, nature is stronger than nurture..

'What shall we do without timber, the last of the woods is down…' We're in Tokyo's Imperial Gardens, a place which contains samples of every single tree species that is to be found in Japan. Have we any such place in Ireland? We'll linger for a while in front of the Suwanochaya, the Tea Pavilion.

Lunch. Eithne says she feels that she is back teaching kindergarten again, the chairs are so low-sized. Afterwards, we head for the Haiku Museum. They give me permission to write the following newly-composed haiku in the visitor's book:

grian trí dhuilliúr…
        an eol don éanlaith
gur i nGairdín an Impire a chanaid?

sun through foliage
do the birds know
they sing in the Emperor's Garden?

I recognise the names of some of the poets who have visited this place already. Canadian haiku poet George Swede, Ion Codrescu from Romania, American J.W.

Hackett and Breton Alain Kervern. I've helped organise readings for all four in Ireland at various junctures, as it happens.

We are reading the Mainichi Weekly, a publication which has an accompanying English-Japanese glossary. The lead story is the plight of the innocent children of Afghanistan. On page eighteen, we read the lyrics of Enya's song "Wild Child". On page twenty is a review of the film Nora, including something which I haven't seen in any newspaper, anywhere—an extract from the film's dialogue:

James: Nora? Oh, there you are hiding. You'll never believe what happened to me.

Nora: I don't give a tinker's curse what happened to you.

This piece of dialogue has an accompanying translation in Japanese. I discover later that there is no reference to the tinker's curse in the Japanese translations. Lost in translation.

Tokyo
commuters
pickled

Celebrated festivals in Tokyo for thee month of September: the Tokyo-to Kiku Matsuri, the Festival of Chrysanthemums; Bunka no Hi, the Day of Culture; Schichi-go-san, a ceremony of prayer for boys aged 3-5 and girls aged 3-7, where their growth towards adolescence is celebrated; Kinro Kansha no Hi, a national holiday for all workers; Tori no Ichi , a festival where people present each other with rakes made from bamboo in the hope that they will rake in money and gold during the course of the year. Have we enough traditional festivals of this type back in Ireland? It would be interesting to make comparative graphs of all the festivals held in Ireland and Japan. Maybe we could have a Thatching Festival and ask Maggie Thatcher to officially launch it?

A grim-faced passenger sits opposite us on the underground train, his face half-hidden by a green anti-pollution mask. He looks like a surgeon preparing for a very complicated operation which he is about to perform on himself. For God's sake, don't do it!

We have dinner on the fifty-first floor of a skyscraper in the company of an old friend of ours, Professor Matsumura, someone who has a great knowledge of Irish literature, the literature of the Old Irish period included.

Gotokuji Temple
chestnut mind
cracks

Tonight we slipped quietly into Japan's secret world, paying a visit to a Zen temple which is dedicated to the cat. A meal afterwards in Fusako's house—shellfish, chicken, shitake mushrooms and many other ingredients all mixed together in one giant pot. The steaming pot is placed in the middle of the table while Professor Fukuda and I recite some haiku. We give some presents to our Japanese hosts and they open them there and then as a sign of their respect for us. In normal circumstances, the Japanese custom is to leave presents unopened while those who have bought them are still present. Do they follow this custom in case the presents prove a disappointment? The wasabi is taking effect. I blow my nose. In fact, this is also an impolite thing to do in Japanese culture. Who knows how many rules of Japanese etiquette we breaking here unknownt to us.

(I remember the time I blew my nose on the street in Delhi, India). The next minute somebody ran up behind me and enquired whether I wanted to buy a dozen handkerchiefs).

Professor Fukuda was born on Sado Island, an island renowned for the fact that Basho wrote a haiku here about the Milky Way (incidentally, this is also the name of the renku group which Professor Fukuda directs). I wrote the following haiku for Professor Fukuda:

faoi Bhealach na Bó Finne
    Éire agus Sadó
an-ghar dá chéile

beneath the Milky Way
Ireland and Japan
very close to each other

The Professor sings a song from his native island and I write another haiku in response:

scáil na sléibhte sa loch
ar Oileán Sádó
agus sna súile seo againne

on Sado Island mountains
reflected in the lake
in our eyes.

It is not by trading information or commodities that different cultures really become familiar with one another; it is rather by arriving at a mutual understanding of the emotional dimensions.

Flicking through the Japanese magazine The Harp 2000, I spot an article in praise of Sean G. Ronan who was Irish Ambassador to Japan at one stage. I knew the Sean well and he was a great help to us when I brought America's leading haiku poet, J.W. Hackett, on a visit to Ireland. Hackett asked Ronan at one stage whether he wrote any haiku himself. "Now and Zen," was Ronan's response.

The Incredible Loneliness of the Gods ... I have a chat with Professor Masazumi Toraiwa, a man who has the appearance of the old master who used to be in that television series Kung Fu. He speaks about the four elements—earth, water, air and fire—and the fifth element, that which binds all four together. I recount some of the folk beliefs which were common amongst rural Irish people until fairly recently—the way that they would call out "Seachain" ("Watch out") to "the good people" (the fairies) as they threw the basin of water in which they had washed their feet out the door. A look of sadness passes over the Professor's face; he thinks to himself for a moment. "Kawa no kamisama doitokure!" he says quietly. This is a reference to a saying he had when he was a child. If he was about to wee into a river, it was necessary to warn the river gods to keep their distance. "O Gods of the river, move out of the way please—or you will get wet!"—is what that phrase means. You'd imagine those gods were fairly wet already, wouldn't you?

We open a bottle of Jameson whiskey and toast the older gods. They're in danger of being forgotten you know, those ancient gods. They like to learn that they haven't been completely overlooked, you know!

Clay of Life...Kyoto... we visit a temple—ourselves and thousands of others. A Zen monk passes, a smile etched on his face. He looks over in my direction momentarily with his glinting button-eyes; these are the same tiger eyes which Blake saw so many years ago. 'In what distant deeps or skies/Burnt the fire in thine eyes?' After our visit to the temple, we follow the narrow winding streets to a place where an exhibition of clay artefacts by Mituyuki Kawase—an artist who was born here in 1933—is taking place. On entering the exhibition we remove our shoes, hunker on the floor and examine a series of glazed artefacts and vessels scattered about the room. White rabbits hopping on a plate, two crawfish on a platter, birds sculpted in snow. Kawase learned his trade from his father. This is no ordinary craftwork but high art at its most intricate and exquisite. The prices reflect this reality, unfortunately; the artefacts here are so expensive we wouldn't even have the price of an eggcup.

Everything in that which is small... We're in Kyoto where our friend Professor Masazumi takes about eighty photos a day with his digital camera. He shows them to us later, on his laptop. Temples...trees...gardens...rocks. Why is it that the Japanese have such a fascination with rocks and stones, I ask the Professor? He is not sure. "Lone rocks in a garden; they are the same as islands in the ocean," he says. Or, to put it another way, those rocks are anchors which permit the mind to enjoy a deeper and calmer form of mediation. We Westerners like to have everything in the frame when we take a photograph. We like to see the entire object. Not so for the Japanese. They might take a photo of just one part of a tree, a photo where the totality of that tree is obscured. They love the simplicity of the individual leaves, the colours which fade or change, green, yellow, red, gold. Branches criss-crossing or entwined, geometric patterns like a Paul Klee line-drawing. Child-like sketches, the outline of one leaf and then…a solitary bird on the tip of a bare branch…as if separate of from the other elements in the picture. Fertility…diversity…the uncertainty of living…life's circle…the four seasons…a ray of sunlight, a silhouette…more rocks and stones…the colour of stone, its texture, its shape. What is a rock? What is a stone? Many moons ago, I wrote a short poem about this conundrum:

Bhí cloch ann uair amháin
tháinig cuileoigín
ní cloch a bhí ann a thuilleadh
ach cloch faoi chuileoigín
ní cuileoigín a bhí ann a thuilleadh
ach cuileoigín ar chloch
d'imigh an cuileoigín
d'fhan an chloch

There once was a stone
a little fly came
it was no longer a stone
but a stone beneath a fly
it was no longer a fly
but a fly on a stone

the little fly flew away
the stone remained

It's no wonder really that it was in Japan that Cha'n developed into Zen-Buddhism and flowered in the way it did. Rocks and stones have a special place in Zen. The same with Shintoism, the indigenous religion, the worship of what is ancient, ancestral, the worship of nature. It is here, in Kyoto, (which was the capital of Japan between 794 and 1192 AD) that various measures were put in place to preserve the environment, to protect the world as we know it—that same Kyoto Protocol which the Americans refused to sign. Let's say it out loud again. The Kyoto Protocol which the Americans refused to sign. Again! The Kyoto Protocol which the Americans refused to sign.

The destruction of the world must be outlawed. We owe it to the people who came before us and to the people who will come after us, the seeds that have yet to take root, the trees that have yet to be planted—we owe it to each and every element—we owe it to every life and every form of life—we owe it to ourselves and to the life we have been given. "More kindness, dear Lord, of the renewing green…" as the poet once said.

Today we are going to visit Hiroshima where we can witness man's destructive power for ourselves. Irish writer Eoghan Ó Tuairisc contemplated this nightmare in his poem Aifreann na Marbh: the word "Hiroshima" always needs saying.

Kyoto is surrounded by hills and the sun is slow to rise here; the same sun is early to bed again. Smoked herring and soba (noodles) for lunch. Since Kyoto is some distance from the sea—and given that it was frequently besieged by its enemies over the centuries—the locals became expert in the smoking of food. No wonder that the place is famous for pickles. The fish is not bitter-tasting; it is the opposite rather, sweet-tasting, floating in the soup. We eat our fish and noodles and we drink the soup, raising the bowl to our lips instead of using a spoon. The waiter bows to us repeatedly as we say goodbye—as is the custom here for a thousand years or more.

Business cards are exchanged between people all of the time here in Japan. If someone offers you their card, it is customary to accept it with both hands held out as a sign of respect—in addition to bowing slightly.

How can one explain the religious philosophy that is Zen in simpler terms? The first thing is not to think of it as an actual religion. In fact don't analyze it at all! Zazen means to sit without thinking. Sit as Buddha sat, not on heavenly clouds but on the earth that forms part of this corrupt world. You have to sit yourself close to the earth...root yourself. ("Become a tree", as Ó Direáin once put it). The Japanese person would have his own reading of Ó Direáin's poem, of course, and think of Basho's 'Go to the pine.').

Do not be an inflexible tree, however. Do not be dour and unyielding. Remain open and malleable. Humble yourself.

On the train to Hiroshima, the ticket-collector makes an appearance in our carriage. He stands erect at the head of the carriage and formally introduces himself before walking from person to person to check the tickets. A ritual of sorts and a nice one at that. Who knows? Maybe when he sits down later for a rest, he'll have a bit of zazen for himself.

To practice zazen solely for oneself is the road to perdition according to Zen philosophy. Zazen should generate an empathy or understanding with the suffering and humanity of the other person—since nobody knows what is going on in another person's mind.

On the train to Hiroshima, I am thinking of the strangeness of this country's culture; some of the people are fairly friendly, others are hostile and you can tell by them that they would prefer not to have outsiders such as ourselves in their midst. My forgetful Professor—Professor Masazumi—asked me whether Irish people know much about Japan. I told him that a frequent stereotype of Japan was that which we found in the English comics as youngsters. (It would be worth someone's while to study the effects of British propaganda on us (in Ireland) over the years, whether in comics, books or films.) I remember that it was the cruelty of the Japanese that was supposed to be their most defining trait according to these comics; particularly the ingenious tortures they invented for prisoners-of-war. I shared one such ‘myth’ with the professor: an unfortunate prisoner is tied naked to a pole, an electric wire right in front of him. They send out this gorgeous scantily-clad woman to dance around in front of him. The poor prisoner becomes aroused and despite his best efforts he is electrocuted... The Professor heaves a sigh that is half-happy and half-sad. He was a teenager during the War years and who knows what he witnessed then? Who knows what he experienced? We leave the subject there and move onto something else. It is a story as yet to be told. An unfinished conversation; it hangs there between us, without beginning or end.

The ticket-collector is finished his work and he stands to attention again at the head of the carriage—as if at the threshold, the very steps of Heaven or Hell. He surveys his passengers once again, knowing he may never see us again in this life or the next, bows and leaves. Imagine that ritual on the train to Westport. The poor ticket-collector would be told to get out at Ballinasloe and have his head examined!

During Zazen, one learns various techniques to calm one’s breathing, to settle the storm that is the mind, to penetrate those stray clouds of delusion. That cloud is considered a form of pollution. In fact, every thought, whether good or bad, is considered a form of defilement. In other words, there are a whole raft of images—whether memory or dream—in the subconscious and they are always trying to break through and present themselves. It is considered good that these images and feelings should make themselves known—it is their right. Much of it is just psychic baggage, meaningless rubbish that we would do better to jettison. That is what zazen is, the casting off of all that mindless rubbish and chatter. Right! Out with you...rubbish! Out you go! What is left when this baggage has been removed? It is our true natures which are revealed—our real selves—prior to the reign of ego.

Do not think of anything. That is what the Zen master Dogen advised. Try it out, anyway. Try not to think of a banana for a moment. Close your eyes. Did you manage to keep the image of a banana from your mind? It is a very difficult thing to do this; in fact, it is downright impossible to practice this exercise without having some form of training in mediation. All of those myriad images which clog up our subconscious; they are like the foam which gathers at the edge of the river; the only way to make them disappear is if we succeed in not focussing on them. A useful precept used within Zen Buddhism is as follows: "If you meet the Buddha on the road, kill him!" That is to say do not travel the journey of life weighed down by an enormous baggage. Jettison it all, and Buddhism too if you have to.

It is not required of the Zen Buddhist that he confess his sins. If he has sinned, then these sins are simply a fog which will disappear beneath the bright sun of zazen. In other words, there is no salvation or grace or forgiveness which comes from the outside. It is by practicing zazen that you come upon your own pure unadulterated likeness, your true nature, your being.

It is when I get to see that refined image of the Buddha from the temple of Zeno—in the Hiroshima Museum of Commemoration—I realize how important this philosophy of peace really is. I think of the bombs currently falling in Afghanistan. Visit Hiroshima and you will be left under no illusions regarding our solemn and human duty to ensure peace spreads throughout the world; everywhere and every how, now and forever.

I'd never want to visit Hiroshima on my own. It is too frightening. We were lucky that we felt somewhat "at home". Our guide is a Japanese girl who learned Irish in Corca Dhuibhne, believe it or not.

The Americans nicknamed the atomic bomb which fell on Hiroshima at 8.15 am on the sixth of August, 1945 Little Boy. That little boy killed 140,000 people. Visit the following site to see how: www.pcf.city.hiroshima.jp

Is it not time that the U.S. made an official apology to the people of Hiroshima for what happened?

We are on our way back to Kyoto—"cridhe lán de smuaintibh" (with much to ponder). Even the girl with the refreshments trolley; she turns and bows to everybody in the carriage before moving onto the next one.

I meet up with the Hailstones. Although you might think it, they are not a pop-group! They are actually a group of haiku poets who meet regularly under the stewardship of Englishman Stephen Gill. We have a haiku session together, a long one where we study twenty newly-composed haiku at one sitting. It becomes a competition of sorts and muggins here finishes second. Leaving the house, I mistakenly put on the wrong pair of shoes. A real Haiku Master would never be so unobservant!

The Temple of Ryoanji in Kyoto. The temple's floorboards are known as uguisi (nightingale); every time you move it makes a melodious creaking, like the chatter of birds. The monks used to fight one another here in medieval times but these cedar boards would betray your presence if you were planning a surprise attack.

Fuji
an iceberg
among clouds

Hundreds gather to visit the Garden of Stones, myself included. I, who grew up on the fertile plains of Munster—the cold and stark nature of stone is not an element of my heritage. No wonder the Japanese are so taken with the Aran Islands when they visit Ireland—"mórchuid cloch is gannchuid cré"/ 'stones a-plenty, earth scarce'.

There are fifteen different types of rock to be seen in the Zen Garden of Ryoanji, each of them positioned on a surface of white gravel. The walls of the Garden are made of clay, a clay that has been boiled hard in oil. The extract from this oil is also what created the unique patterns on the walls. Who would have thought it! Aran writer Dara Ó Conaola has written a short story in which a stone speaks. I see now that certain academics are trying to make links between the tradition of animism in Ireland and a similar animist tradition as found in Japan

(Celt to Nippon). It looks as if there is definitely a subject worth studying there. In reality, the word "animism" isn't mentioned half often enough during discussions of Gaelic culture.

The fashion, pop music and film industries of the West have an enormous influence on present-day Japan. Currently, the fashion here amongst young people is for the dyeing of hair; give it a few years and there will be some people genetically manipulating their eyes—so that their eyes will be shaped more like Caucasians. With this depressing thought in mind, we head for Australia. It is rumoured that there is a notice of welcome on entering Australia that admonishes us to EAT MORE BEEF YOU BASTARDS.

It is a while since I looked at newspaper. In the International Herald Tribune there is an article by one Alice Feiring outlining how the events of September the eleventh have affected the champagne business. Apparently, champagne is only drunk at weddings now in America. Doesn't she have little enough to be worried about!

Our next port of call is Randwick, a suburb of east Sydney that's within a kangaroo's grunt of Coogie Beach, a beach that is never as crowded as Bondi by all accounts. I thought first that the word Coogie might possibly have come from an immigrant Irish person, somebody homesick who was recalling the word "cúige"/ 'province' in their new country. This was just a shot in the dark. It turns out that "coogie" is an Aboriginal word. The Aborigines have made Australia their home for more than 50,000 years. As a point of comparison, the Irish have been in Ireland for only 7000 years or so. Coogie is a word which means "a smelly (foul) place". Haven't we a place in Ireland which is known as Bréantrá? (Literally, evil-smelling beach). Don't ask me where it is. Wait! I know where it is: it's in County Cork and it's known as Unionhall in the Queen's English. The smell of rotten seaweed is what gave it its name. The name Chicago (shikaakwa) also stands for "smelly place" but they blamed the skunk for the smell there. Or was it a pungent form of onion? One way or the other, I see no Aborigines around Randwick, unfortunately.

Botany Bay (which gets a mention or two in Irish history) isn't far from Sydney. It's here that Captain Cook first set foot in Australia, in April 1770. He wrote a vivid description of the indigenous people upon his arrival:

> They may appear to some to be the most wretched people upon the earth: but in reality they are far more happier than we Europeans; being wholly unacquainted not only with the superfluous but the necessary Conveniences so much sought after in Europe, they are happy in not knowing the use of them. They live in a Tranquility which is not disturbed by the Inequality of Condition; The Earth and Sea of their own accord furnishes them with all things necessary for life; they covet not Magnificent Houses, Household stuff etc.; they live in a warm and fine Climate and enjoy a very wholesome Air: so that they have very little need of Clothing and this they seem to be fully sensible of for many to whome we gave Cloth etc. left it carelessly upon the Sea beach and in the woods as a thing they had no manner of use for. In short they seemed to set no value upon anything we gave them nor would they ever part with any thing of their own for any one article we could offer them...
>
> (A Short History of Australia)

We have something to eat in the Barzura, a restaurant which looks out over the sea—the same sea that transported convicts and colonizers to New South Wales—the 'Connerys' of the memorable song amongst them. We both order gemfish, a bright pearl of baked fish that we've never heard of before. We'd try out kangaroo too, only it isn't on the menu.

The place-names of Australia are fascinating. Inverell, for example. Was it a Gael who, running out of names, called the place Inbhear Eile ('Another Estuary')? No. Though it is Irish, Inbhear Eala or Inbhear Ealaí, ('Estuary of Swans'). Who knows whether it was a white swan or a black swan that the Irish, or Scots-Gaelic person, named it after but no matter; it's a fine name nonetheless. If the British made a hash of Irish-language names in Ireland rendering them meaningless and unintelligible, the Gaels of Ireland and Scotland imposed the same form of colonization in Australia, altering the meaning of indigenous names such as "Giree Giree" ("the high-banked river") to Inverell—to give but one such example. A man by the name of Rev. Seán Flynn recorded the following indigenous name in his papers—Warrawarrapiraliliullamalulacoupalunmya! But do you think he bothered to tell us what it meant? Many of the Aboriginal dialects declined and died—at the same time as tribes were evicted from their tribal lands—long before scholars had any opportunity to record the etymologies of the many thousands of placenames and the rest of the lore.

Today they think that the name "Amaroo" is a reference to "abar rua" (red bog, red mud) while Ardlethan was named after a place in Scotland called Ard Leathan. Ballan (Ballán) was given its name by an Irishman named Robert von Steiglitz (!), who named it after his homeplace back in Ireland.

Not my type of guy, von Steiglitz, who recorded the following in his diary:

> '... it may be questioned by some feather-bed philanthropist whether we had the right to take the country from the blacks but I believe the general rule is that if people cultivate or graze the land they have a claim to it. These creatures did neither ...'

There are so many stories hidden beneath placenames words and names but the curious scholar would be researching till Judgement Day, the place-names are by now so occluded within history. You would begin by seeking links between the Aborginal words and the syllables and sounds of other languages, Irish included, and "therein lies madness", as someone once said. Barrawatha, for example. What does this mean? Is it "barr an bhata"—"the top of the stick"? Is it a reference to some rough type of boomerang? Maybe—although the experts here say that it refers to the phrase "deaf and dumb". OK. What about this one—Beal Ba? Add the necessary accents and we get Béal Bá (mouth of bay/ mouth of drowning?) Could be... We're making progress here!

Australia is a land of immigrants and there are people here from every corner of the world. The humour here is multicultural as a consequence: An American, a Russian and an Israeli are sitting in a restaurant when the waiter approaches them:

"I'm sorry," he says. "Unfortunately, there is a scarcity of meat at the moment."

"What does scarcity mean?", the American asks.

"What is meat?" the Russian asks.

Hard to bring to mind, all those prospectors and adventurers who came here, the English and Irish people who were deported in their thousands—their amazement on seeing the incredible diversity of this land for the first time, albeit the beauty of the landscape was hardly to the forefront of their minds upon arrival.

Coogie: lager-white waves
A surfer rides
a yellow board

And what about the terrible struggles those first arrivals endured, the same poor creatures who gave the name Nowhere Else when asked the question, "Where will this road lead me?" The same people wouldn't have had the slightest interest, of course, in the indigenous placenames they found—the likes of Eucla, for instance, a place which means "the bright flash"—in reference to the fact that Venus rises lucidly above the freshwater dunes.

We put the News on in the Randwick Lodge. The Pope issues an apology to the Australian Aborigines on behalf of the West. One of the most brutal practices the white colonists indulged in is not mentioned, however. This was the cruel "game" where Aborigines were buried in sand up to their necks and their heads used as rugby balls—for kicking practice.

An advertisement in Bondi Beach: Fruitologist. Some type of psychologist maybe? No, it is simply a reference to someone who sells fruit—a fruitseller.

The weather is beautiful today and we decide to go the races in Randwick. A horse shits in the parade ring. "That's the one that'll win!" says Eithne. And sure enough, that horse does prove the winner. I don't enjoy the race meeting at all. There is something strange about this race-course, something antiseptic or clinical, something mechanistic even. A large number of race meetings from throughout Australia come beaming from a giant screen in the middle of the racecourse. There is too much happening here—too much going on. I recognise the names of one or two famous sires on the race-card—Royal Academy and Danehill included—but this is no help to me in trying to work out who might win. Eithne's approach is still the best. The horse who shits first will win.

This place doesn't have the atmosphere you'd normally expect at a race meeting. A man collecting rubbish is up in the stand. Proper order is maintained here and the madness that one associates with a real race meeting is curiously absent. Alas! I've already blown a hundred Australian dollars (by the time the fourth race begins). It's time for us to leave Royal Randwick and get some sense. There will be no miracle today. I think back to the old days, those days I spent on the racecourses of Ireland, Thurles racecourse amongst them. I believed in miracles in those bygone days. Of course, racing was very different back then, in every way; they were much rougher occasions; the crowd noisier and more mixed, the bookies more colourful. The first monkey I ever saw—and I'm not referring to the racecourse lingo here (i.e. £500 pounds) was not in any zoo. It was sitting on the shoulder of well-known bookmaker Terry Rogers. That was the Ireland of the past, the oppressed Ireland of poverty and the emigrant boat, and it was no surprise that gambling had a touch of madness about it then. The most resourceful of the bookies used to have a sign held high in those days—Minimum Bet £5. Some of the less well-off bookies had the look which said: "You can bet a turnip on the favourite if that's all you have!"

éan maidine, Coogie –
a ghlór ná a chleití
ní aithním

Coogie morning bird
what are you
your feathers … your voice …

Back then, I would know I had made it to manhood when I was able to put down a £5 bet on a horse. In between-times, I had to make do with my shiny half-crown. I picked out a horse named Ark's Fancy, my brothers sniggering in the background. "That's not a horse that you picked; it's a mule". I'll bet you can get 25/1 on that slowcoach! And look who's the trainer! A farmer! He's not a real trainer, at all sonny! And as far as the jockey is concerned, God help us! There'll be no problem about him staying in the saddle; he's that heavy. That's about the only good thing you could say about him!"

I left them where they were skitting and laughing and went off to do my own thing. I remember coming to the stalls that sold chocolate, oranges and pears. I was tempted but there was no way I was letting go of that half-crown of mine— and the fine horse that was chiselled on the coin. I kept my hands in my pockets and felt the coin regularly—in case any pickpocket would swipe it unknown to me. There were plenty of pickpockets there that day—they will always be there, I suppose. I can't remember now exactly which race meeting we were at that afternoon—maybe it was Thurles? It was cloudy, you see; there was rain on the wind. Was it Mallow maybe?—the racetrack that they now call Cork. Or maybe it was Limerick Junction, a race meeting they now call Tipperary Races. I can't be sure, it was that long ago. The place was thronged with people. Don't ask me why, but at one stage, I felt somebody was watching me and I took a quick glance over my shoulder. A tall red-haired man was following me. I was sure of it. This man was no pickpocket. He was one of the gentry; I could tell by the way he was dressed. One of the racing circle, a man with a long coat and a hat, one of those people who would sit in the stand at every big race meeting up and down the country. He had the look of wealth about him. Or some other look that I couldn't quite put my finger on. I broke into a run. Weaving my way through the crowd, I tried to lose him. At one stage I took a quick glance over my shoulder and to my horror the man was still following me! The word 'paedophile' wasn't a term that was well-known in those days but I sensed that this man had something about him that was not quite right; there was something evil in his intentions towards me. There wasn't much he could do to me, of course, if I stayed in the middle of the crowd here, in broad daylight. When you are a child and you are frightened you don't think of these things of course, you simply run. Unknown to me, I had completed a circle of the area and was back close to where my mother was; I spotted her leopard-skin coat in the crowd and ran towards it. "Mam…" I said when I got as far as her, grabbing a hold of the leopard-skin. I looked back over my shoulder. The man backed off and turned away, he disappeared into the crowd. I breathed a huge sigh of relief and turned back to the leopard-skin. It wasn't my mother at all! A heavily-made up woman was stared down angrily at me.

"What do you want?" she said, abruptly.

"Who do you think will win the third race?" I said.

Years later I was watching a television documentary about Arkle, the legendary racehorse. Some of the documentary was filmed in black-and-white, that was how old it was. They showed a scene of a group of the Irish racing fraternity, roaring on Arkle as he ran in to win the Cheltenham Gold Cup of 1965. My heart stood still! There he was…standing in the middle of the crowd, the man who had pursued me so many years before. He was old and decrepit-looking…he had the look of a man who was well over one hundred years of age. That strange man—he would be dead and gone years ago by now. I'll say no more about him.

Back to that day again so many years ago…back to when I was still a child. I remember hearing the tannoy system call out the result of the previous race.

"Winner alright, Winner all right. Tote, Win: One pound, ten shillings and sixpence." Place:..."

It was all sweet music to my ears! It won't be long now before the next race, a three-mile steeplechase, I think to myself and I make my way to the parade ring to get a quick look at the horses before the serious betting men gather en masse and crowd out the enclosure. Some of the racing fraternity have already gathered there, those seasoned race-goers who attend every single meet no matter where it is…up and down the country. Race-card in hand, they eye up the circling horses carefully. The horses have a solemnity about them as they are led quickly around the enclosure by the white-coated stable-hands. In the centre of the ring, the owners and trainers are already huddled together in their Sunday best; their faux-English accents ringing out. Posh accents and country accents melded together in strange symphony. And if a horse was to shit there and then beside them, it wouldn't knock a stir out of them, they who are in their fine suits and shined shoes. These are the hunting fraternity, after all. Somebody behind them says: "He's sweatin' up a bit" (normally, a bad sign in a horse) but the huddled group barely turn or take notice. One or two horses have bandaged forelegs. Round and round they go. The jockeys in their silks. Blue, black and yellow. The jockey spots the owner's wife or daughter and he performs a gentle curtsy before her, acknowledging her presence. The racing women, finely turned out in their hats and feathers, they close ranks like the men, they examine their race-cards. Talking about likely tactics, which horse might be a frontrunner, which one had the stamina and the like. Who'd hold back and wait for the home straight? Who'd win the race if their own horse didn't?

A boot tests the ground to see how soft it is. The bell sounds; the rider takes hold of the reins, a foot in the stirrup, he's hoisted aboard. Some last-minute advice from the trainer as the jockey settles into the saddle. Majestic, masterful. One more circuit of the parade ring. The announcement: The horses are leaving the parade ring…

My brothers turn out to be right in the end. You could have got odds of 25/1 - or better—on Ark's Fancy. He didn't look like much when he was in the parade ring, his head down, as if uninterested in the proceedings taking place around him. My mind's not for changing, however. There are long queues in front of the Tote as I take my place in the line. My chance comes finally. "Win No. 11 please…". Ticket in hand, I make my way back to the viewing stand. Finally I have a ticket of my own…One of my brother swipes the ticket out of my hand. "Win No. 11!" he says and he bursts out laughing.

"The white flag is raised…".

"They're off!"

It's a three-miler. Eighteen fences. My mule is last; he's holding up the rear as they pass the stand. Two miles later and Ark's Fancy almost falls. His hind legs clatter hard against one of the jumps but hats off to rider! He stays aboard. Any other jockey would have hit the ground straight away with a bruised behind for a week. My hero of a jockey is glued to the saddle, however. He straightens up and keeps on going. Before we know it, they have just three fences left to jump. Just five horses from the original eleven are left in the running. A horse that had odds of 8/1 on him is out in front but the favourite is coming on strong. A roar emerges from the belly of the crowd as the favourite makes his charge for home.

Where is my fella? He's in fifth place, trailing the rest of the field by a good thirty lengths. The next fence and there are two fallers. The leader goes first. Then the favourite who was steaming up behind him, crumbless on top of the leader…a chorus of jeers rises up from the crowd at this turn of events.

What next? The horse which is now in the lead looks out on his feet. Incredible as it may seem… he refuses point-blank at the next jump. He's had enough. Now there are just two horses left in the running, neither of which had a hope-in-hell just minutes before. There isn't a gig out of any of us, a look of incredulity on our faces. My brother looks over at me, his mouth wide with shock. "He could do it yet—your one." They come to the second-last fence and my fella is ten yards in front! They are on the run-in now, neck-and-neck as they approach the last. The other horse pulls slightly ahead but his breathing is heavy. He's running out of steam, there's not much left in the tank. One hundred yards left to run and instead of passing on the outside as he should, what does my jockey do but make as if to go for the inside? He makes for the rails but it breaks the horse's stride. He loses at least a length with that tactic.

"What in the devil's name is he doing?" I cry out and my child's mind clouds with suspicion. Maybe he's taken a bribe to let the other horse win?

"He's brought him into the rails," says my brother in a conspiratorial voice, gripping me by the elbow, "he's done that to keep him straight on the run-in." My brother is right, that is exactly what the rider is doing…and, incredibly, it seems to work! The sight of his rival on the inside seems to disorient the other horse completely. He is dizzy with exhaustion and he is staggering all over the place. My brothers and I whoop with delight as my horse strides past the finishing line. We must be the only people in this enormous crowd—the bookies excepted –who shout out with delight. Arks Fancy is the unlikely hero of the hour. I jump for joy. I am the king.

My brothers and I still talk about that race, even today. It's one of those "lines" we use amongst ourselves when we are having a bit of crack. Any time one of us is seeking a miracle, all we do is mention "Ark's Fancy"! And miracles do happen! Maybe they are rare, but they do happen! And one of those miracles is that I would later give up gambling. Not that I regret having had addictions. The addictive, compulsive personality is really in search of Truth, Beauty and Self-Realization, whether he knows it or not. You can bet your bottom dollar on that…

Aboriginal art is beautiful to look at. Many of the Aboriginal artists have Irish surnames which makes it even more fascinating—names like Mulcahy, for example. Their paintings are outstanding and they have magical titles to go with them. A Hunting Crocodile; Turtles' Resting-Place, patterns which are both abstract and modern you might say—on an initial glance. This style is as old as the mists of time, however.

One question which has always intrigued me. At a time when so many other indigenous peoples and groups were experiencing rapid change, how was it that the Aborigines stayed much the same? Was it because their cosmology was what it was, complete, that nothing could be added to it, except another tale, another picture which was simply another decorative way of saying the same thing, expressing the same vision? And since there wasn't a great variety of animals (as seed carriers), the land was not cultivated, property was unknown.

In India we saw temples dedicated to the elephant-god, Ganesh and to the monkey-god, Hanuman. As chance would have it, similar temples were never built in Australia—dedicated to the kangaroo-god, say—though the Hindus and Buddhists of southern India did once plan to colonize Australia. What derailed this plan was the Moslem invasion of India in the 1500s.

Consider it for a moment. If Hindus and Buddhists had arrived, Australia might be a completely different country today—a country without beef, alcohol or gambling. The kangaroo—(re-named something else, of course) would be free to bound and shit wherever he wished. What would the Mumbai woman have to say about that then? She'd have no problem with the possibility of a kangaroo deity, I'm sure. There is a god within the kangaroo. That much is certain. God must jump after all! You didn't think he stood stock-still (and in the one place) all of the time, now did you?

The Chinese never succeeded in colonizing Australia any more than the Indians did. It took a while for the Europeans themselves to make it as far as Australia, the South Sea tides kept sweeping them away from the landmass that was Australia—pushing them ever northwards.

blue flowers of the jacaranda –
look!
a sulphur-crested cockatoo

In Sydney Aquarium a group of German tourists try to catch a glimpse of the duck-billed platypus

"Wo ist der Kerl?" (Where is he, the rogue?)

"Versteckt!

He's hidden beneath a tree-stump.

"Da ist er!" (There he is!)

Suddenly, he sticks out his gob. The duck-billed platypus. It's himself! The platypus is a graceful swimmer but he's not too elegant when he's on dry land; awkward, he bangs into things. He's a bit like us—bumping into these duck-billed Germans.

A dead duck-billed platypus was first sent as a specimen to Britain in the year 1798. The scientists there burst out laughing when they saw it for the first time. They thought it was some kind of a hoax!

This is how people's poet "Banjo" Paterson (author of Waltzing Matilda described the platypus:

And he talks in a deep unfriendly growl
As he goes on his journey lonely;
For he's no relation to fish or fowl,
Nor to bird nor beast, nor to hornéd owl"
In fact, he's the one and only!

You can't discuss the history of the poetry journal INNTI without mentioning the journal which preceded it—Motus—and here in Sydney I meet up with Roderic Campbell, an old friend and the man who founded Motus. He's lived in Rozelle, Sydney, for many years now where he works as a translator and editor, just as I have done myself. I have a feeling he's always falling out with authors; he may think he knows more than they do about whatever book he happens to be editing and, well, he probably does. Why hasn't literary or even commercial success come his way? Somebody should write A Book of Solace for the thousands of writers who, for one reason or another, are outside of the Pale. Gaelic Ireland lived outside of the Pale. Some would argue that nothing has changed.

Campbell is two Gaelic words, cam meaning crooked, or wry, and béal, mouth. Roderic had a wryness to him that few of us had ever seen before. Was he suffering from post-Glencoe trauma?

It's twilight beneath the jacaranda trees in Roderic's back garden. Torch in hand, he goes in search of a cicada.

"The cicada lives under the ground for seven years," he tells me. There's a bit of the cicada about Roderic himself. When we were at university together in Cork he kept many of us alive with such encyclopaedic nuggets. I was a priest in his production of a Noh play. Heady stuff. There was nothing the groves of academe could do to compete with that, even if they wanted to. He first introduced me to the writings of R.H. Blyth, opening the doors to the amazing universe of haiku. Where can one find words to express gratitude? Simply by writing haiku, I imagine.

He can't find a live cicada right now but he shows me the tiny skull of a dead one.

"I was working on a book about insects there recently and next thing my study was invaded by scores of insects. They were all there swarming around the computer screen. One of them pissed on me..."

Does a cicada actually urinate? Hey...who am I to question Roderic's knowledge in these matters...he's the man with the torch, illuminating the darkness of the garden, the darkness of his gifted mind.

Weren't half the students in Cork afraid of his 'Nosferatu, Phantom der Nacht', presence? The tall silk hat perched on a head, crammed with arcane knowledge. The walking cane, his protection against the ignorant of the world. The Guards pulled him over more than once during those years.

"What's your name and what's your business walking around this city at the dead of night?"

"Oh," he'd say, "it's looking for my stray camels I am, Garda. They've wandered off somewhere into the loneliness."

Roderic claims to have learned nothing from his time at University.

"We had a Capuchin who was trying to teach us about epistemology and he had this habit of stopping in mid-sentence and staring at the back of the room while rubbing his hand across his forehead. We couldn't understand what was going through his mind at all. It turns out that he thought he could see Thomas Aquinas sitting at the back of the classroom. Then there was Séan Lucy our English lecturer who spent far too much time trying to prove that Shakespeare was a Catholic..."

Out in the Blue Mountains...125 kilometres west of Sydney. It is the gas which escapes from the eucalyptus tree which has coloured the mountains blue.

Australia has more than 700 different species of eucalyptus tree and it isn't every type of eucalyptus leaf that the koala bear will feed on— no fear of it—and there are only 35 different species of that little bear in Australia. It is estimated that the koala bear population of Australia is about 80,000 in total.

Herbalist's Secret... There was a species of pine tree in Australia once which was known as the Wollemi; it is thought to have become extinct about 150 million years ago. Imagine the joy of all herbalists then when scientists came across a living specimen of the Wollemi tree in 1994. The word "Wollemi" means "be aware of your surroundings"; there is a lot of truth in the name as this is a very remote area of the world; one could easily get lost here and never be found again.

the tiny mynah bird
makes such a racket
he frightens the raven away

The general public have not been told where this rare specimen of the Wollemi tree is being kept. We're not allowed see it either!

The thirtieth of November proves the longest day yet—since leaving Ireland behind two months earlier—on the thirtieth of September. We travel for more than twelve hours to Auckland, New Zealand where the only thing we see is a person wearing a
T-shirt emblazoned with the words "I support the New Zealand team and any team which is playing against Australia". A journey of more than 10,000 kilometres to Buenos Aires in Argentina awaits us. There is a time difference of 16 hours between both countries so that although we leave Auckland on Friday afternoon, we arrive in Buenos Aires around lunch-time the same day.

In the pizzeria, the waitress—wearing the shortest black skirt the world has ever seen—asks us where we are from. It takes me a moment to think where I'm from—Irlanda!

"Oh, I know it well, she says—Orlando". I momentarily consider correcting her geography but decide it's a waste of time; I might as well be talking to Maggie Thatcher.

"Si, si, Orlando!" The woman tells us all about her brothers who live in the US. One of them just had a new baby. "He's just a month old!" We need to get a drink of water quick. "Sin gas, I say, no fizz.. I feel about a hundred years of age, I am so wrecked. This Friday seems to be the longest Friday in living memory.

What has brought us to South America? We are going to meet my father's only brother—Curt—on Sunday. We're going to meet up in Santiago de Chile. I have cousins there whom I've never met in my life. What kind of people are they? Will we all get on well together?

Roses über alles... Am I the only Rosenstock in Buenos Aires at this present moment? I check out the phone book. Oh...look. There are two. The prefix Rosen seems to be fairly common here alright...Rosenblut, the blood of the roses. Isn't that a beautiful name. Rosenvasser, rose-water and a host of others: Rosenbaum, Rosenberg, Rosenblatt, Rosendorn, Rosenfarb, Rosengarten, Rosenkrantz, Rosenzweig...Most of them are Jewish, I take it. It wouldn't surprise me if there was a Rosenlobster here, there are so many Rosens...

What will we do tomorrow? We don't know a soul in this place. There are a few Irish bars here but...we mightn't bother with them this time. It's probably better to spend some time reading and writing and catching up on some sleep.

It is the smallest and the strangest of things which bind people and places together. Malgudi Days includes a short story named Emden. The Emden was the name of a German warship which attacked the Indian city of Madras (Chennai) in that fateful year of 1916. For years afterwards, and maybe today in certain parts of India, the word Emden meant somebody who was rough, a violent person, a person who was without mercy. In Australia, I read a book entitled A Short History of Australia by Manning Clark, a person who had a very strange view of Irish Catholics, in my opinion. And what did I read in that book—only that the Emden was sent to its watery grave off the Coco Islands by an Australian destroyer named The Sydney. What a strange coincidence—literature, folklore and history all meeting one another, in my mind at least.

The hotel here in Buenos Aires is fairly basic and goes by the name of Sarmiento Suites. The breakfast room has only one picture on the wall, a painting of a flowering cactus by Georgia O'Keefe. It is an eerie celebration of the feminine, of unrestrained sexuality (if I'm not mistaken). It says a good deal about the Latin-American culture in which we now find ourselves. The same with the bedrooms and the hotel corridors. Pictures of plants decorate the walls. I look forward to meeting my close relatives—will their Chilean nature be more evident in them than their German-culture inheritance? After all, my own parents were half-tempted to emigrate to Chile also after the Second World War had come to an end. Curt had already emigrated by then; he'd had gone on ahead of them having left Germany for a new life over there even before the War had broken out at all. If fate had taken that twist I'd be a Hispanic today. Maybe I would never have laid eyes on Ireland at all? Curt's sons have never been to Ireland yet. If things had taken a different turn my sole connection with Ireland might be something as tenuous as that of Chilean patriot, Bernardo O'Higgins? And which fool would poor Eithne take on and marry if I wasn't here? All of these strange twists and turns...they would set you thinking alright...la vida es sueño, life is but a dream. True or not?

Maggie Thatcher, if you happen to read this, I'd just like you to know that Eithne and I are at this moment standing at the memorial to all the Argentines who were killed in the Malvinas War—or the Falklands War as you would have it. Eithne blesses herself as a sign of respect. Does she do this in order to demonstrate to the two sailors who guard the memorial that she is not English? No. She has just said a prayer for all of the mothers who lost their children, all of the mothers whose sailor children were brutally shuttled to eternity.

La Nación…....the newspaper La Nación has a poetic headline: La Guitarra Iloró por Harrison...the Guitar weeps for George Harrison. Strange how stories appear when you are abroad. Perspectives shift. Amongst the people keening George is the Queen of England, or "La reina Isabel II de Inglaterra...". Isabel, no less!

It was at Irish college in Ballybunion that I first heard tell of the Beatles. We were in class where we learning a rollicking song Amhráinín Síodramín at the time. I'm not sure how many of us understood the words. One of the Beatles' songs was the subject of conversation—in low voices—in the schoolyard. (Ah...now if it had only been the other way round and Amhráinín Síodramín was the topic of our hushed, excited conversation).

The bhakti tradition previously alluded to, an exquisite tradition which I value as I value my heart, was what moulded George Harrison's great song, "My Sweet Lord". Watch him talking about the soul on www.nondualitymagazine.org/ May he find himself in Vrindaban, in the company of Krishna.

We visit the house where the writer Jorge Luis Borges lived. It took us an hour to find it. The newspaper-seller tells us that he knew Borges' wife. The only sign that Borges lived here is the plaque on the wall outside. Sometimes, I feel exactly as Borges felt—those lines he expressed in his autobiography as follows:

> "When something is written that is hostile to me, not only do I agree with it; I also find myself thinking that I could make a much better job of it, myself."

It is the first of December and the heat is brutal. Back we go to the city's main park in search of some shade; we have a new-found respect for leaves. The city's dogs lope around the place, their tongues lolling. Kids are playing in the heat; a girl is thrown into a fountain. Inside the city cathedral there is the mausoleum of General San Martín. The solemn ritual that is the changing of the guard, soldiers dressed in a style reminiscent of a child's toy soldiers. The squeak of boots on the cold slabs of the cathedral. For a moment I think a coup d'état is about to take place.

There are sights in this cathedral which you won't see in many other places. A statue of Jesus, his hands bound, which two well-known soccer players presented to the cathedral. The statue is kept behind a glass which has a special opening so that people can reach in and touch the purple robe of the Saviour. I put my hand through the opening. Why not?

Graffiti on the walls around town urging us to resist CIA domination. We'll do our best. Curt is nearly eighty-eight years of age and lives with his partner Hannelore in a beautiful glen named Maipo, a place known for the quality of its vineyards and wines. There are flowers and a Welcome card awaiting us when we arrive at the house—Wilkommen in Chile. Hannelore, who has been widowed twice is always laughing… not because she laughs at every little thing, but because she is constantly teaching Chileans to pronounce the 'H' in her name,"Ha Ha Ha! Hannelore!". And they respond by dropping the 'H' and adding an 'N', it's driving her crackers: "A-A-A-Annaloren" She'll give up the laughing one of these days, she assures us!

They bring us out for a meal to an unusual restaurant in San José de Maipo. The restaurant, known as Casa Bosque, is constructed entirely of carved wood. At an initial glance, it's like one of those houses you would see in a fairy tale, one of those lonely houses in the woods. "Hubsch, nicht?" Curt says. Pretty, eh? He speaks Spanish, English and German…and sometimes, a mixture of all three in the same sentence. A bit of Portuguese running through it. Also a linguistic stew of Portuguese and Spanish that is almost a new language, Portuñol. Curt isn't a bit happy with the food, however, the tuna is only half-cooked. He has a good mind to swipe the salt cellar when we leave, he says—as compensation for the disappointing meal.

in the fountain a pigeon bathes,
a nun
fingering her beads

The people of Chile are a bit lazy, he says. Too lazy to cook the tuna properly? I get the sense that he feels the country would be better off if he and other Germans were running it! Is it this same laziness he alludes to which results in "mucha gracia" which we hear a lot, as opposed to "muchas gracias"?

Eithne and I don't care one way or the other about the meal. We are so happy to see Curt so sprightly and full of the joys of life. He happily relates to us a number of stories about the years he spent living in Brazil where a German neighbour of his kept a three-legged cockerel! Another person he knew there was able to use a fish which emitted enough electricity to light up a bus, if I am understanding what Curt is saying correctly.

Although Curt says he voted for the Communist candidate Allende, his working life did not blossom under that administration and so he spent thirteen years living in the east, in Brazil. I don't know that I'll ever find out exactly what he did for a living while in Brazil. I do know that he spent some time working in a business which made musical fountains—music and water spouting together. He has a fine garden around his house and a very wide range of plants, healing herbs amongst them.

> "Any idea what kind of a plant that one there is?" Curt asks, pointing towards one of them.
>
> "Haven't a clue", I reply. He breaks off a small twig from it. "That is the quillay, or what is known as the soap plant. Fifty years ago, we used to export this plant to Germany. Its leaves are used to make both soap and shampoo. And that tree over there…that's the eucalyptus. You heat the oil of the eucalyptus and, when inhaled, the steam is very good for the lungs."

There has always been a great demand for tropical plants in Germany.

Curt tells me that my own father used to import such plants to Ireland years ago, a piece of family history that I wasn't aware of.

I had known that my father had an enormous range of interests and had even had a few crackpot schemes "on the go" in his day, most of which came to naught, but I hadn't been aware of this particular sideline.

We drive past one of the musical fountains he was involved in manufacturing years ago. It's a sorry sight; no water, no music; the only thing it emits is a dirty steamy fug.

"Ah…all the internal workings are gone", sighs Curt. "Everything…swiped by the bandidos !".

A political poster on a wall depicts a half-bald politician and a cartoon of a lion beneath his photo. His mantra is: te defiende como león—(he will defend you like a lion). And there is a great need for lion-like defenders of civilization in South America, of that there is no doubt. Curt keeps a close watch out as he parks his car because if your car is stolen here you definitely won't see it ever again. Before you know it, it'll be broken down into its relevant parts each of which will be quickly sold off.

A Ship Came from Valparaiso…Nearly every Irish person of my generation learned that poem by Gogarty, or I should say its beautiful rendition into Irish by Monsignor de Brún, 'Tháinig long ó Valparaiso'.

We visit Jochen's house (Curt's son) in Viña del Mar where we have a night-time view of the cityscape that is Valparaiso, a city founded by the Spaniards in 1536. Not one drop of rain has fallen on this entire region within the past month and 500 kilometres northwards is a Chilean desert, a place where rain hasn't fallen for donkey's years. It's the driest place in the world apparently. Jochen works as a surgeon and when we meet him he's full of chat about the Freemasons. I explain to him that for historical reasons, we Irish have had little truck with the Masons

"But wasn't Goethe a Mason?" he asks. "And Mozart. Do you not like Mozart? "

"I do but…" He turns to his wife Monica and tells her in Spanish that we have strange ideas. One thing which this journey has taught me is that the Catholic cultural inheritance which I received at various schools and taught by nuns, Franciscans, Holy Ghost Fathers and, of course, by my mother, this Catholic culture—whatever about its belief systems– is still a strong influence on my reactions to certain situations that test one's values. It doesn't how deep or transforming my contact may have been with other religious traditions—those of the East, the bhakti tradition and Advaita in particular, culturally I cannot be other than the product of a Catholic upbringing. This doesn't mean that I cannot absorb the cultural, spiritual and psychological delights of Zen, Sufism, Daoism etc. and even anthologise some of their treasures in Irish-language renditions. Anyway, catholic as I may be, this time with a small 'c', I'm not going to join the Masons, in Valparaiso or anywhere else. They can forget it!

Having said that, if I were in Jochen's shoes and keen on advancing myself professionally, who knows?...I might be tempted to become a Freemason and take part in their Scottish rituals at the Masonic lodge of Valparaiso—maybe, the legendary Gobán Saor, as his name suggests, was a Freemason, bless him.

Jochen and his fellow-Masons were worried when Allende first came to power in Chile. Around this time, 10,000 Cuban soldiers arrived in Chile. "Kommunismus? Nein, Vandalismus!" says Jochen (there's no need to translate that). As I've already mentioned, Curt left for Brazil. Jochen went to Germany. He was a happy man when Pinochet came to power. There was order and regulation in the country once more. Well…I tell Jochen quite frankly that I'd find it next to impossible to have any respect for Pinochet, a butcher if ever there was one.

The word "strus" in Irish has two meanings. One implies "tension" or "stress"; the other means "wealth". I suppose the two go together and I see examples in Chile of this. (And stress from lack of money, of course, as well as too much of it). Isn't the pursuit of wealth an awful curse really? You spend half of your life trying to add to your store of money and the other half trying to keep a hold of it and show it off, when the occasion demands.

My father was a big enough fish in a small pond for a while, a bigwig in Kilfinane, County Limerick, where we grew up and I can recall one incident in particular which brought home to me the lack of justice which often accompanies wealth or societal privilege. Myself and a friend of mine named Martin were struck with a bout of "Republican fervour" and we wrote "Brits Out" on a local road in bright paint. The local Garda sergeant duly paid us a visit the next day!

"It's not that I disagree with what you are saying…at all," he said, "it's just that what you did was against the law. And anyway, it might be interpreted as though you wanted local British people out when we all know what you meant is the soldiers in the North…"

To be honest, I never understood for the life of me how he found out we were the graffiti artists! Was poor Martin given a hiding before spilling the beans? Did he squeal on me? All of these thoughts ran through my mind while the Sergeant was in our house that day.

"You'll have to clean it off the road," he said. I gave him a cheeky look. "I'm not cleaning up that!" I said to him and slammed the door shut on him. Wasn't I a right little arrogant son-of-a-gun back then? Part of me wanted to be imprisoned for my actions, martyred even! Where do we get our notions from! Has it something to do with Christian iconography? Did I want to be crucified?

The next day my father had to go into Limerick and I accompanied him in the car. I was hoping to buy a few books in the Treaty Bookstore. Strange treasures had I found there in he past, the letters of the poet Cowper and what not. Who was out on the road as we passed along but Martin, scrubbing the paint away with a brush and a bucket of water. The sweat was pouring off him and he gave me one hell of a dirty look as we swanned by in the Jaguar. "Was macht der Junge? Ist er verrückt?" my father asked me. "What's that young fella doing? Is he out of his mind?" (If my father suspected anyone of being verrückt he would always resort to the language of Freud). I let on of course that I didn't know who Martin was at all.

"A complete nutter, by the looks of it..." I said, but inside I was torn with self-disgust.

breeze rustles in the garden
the Alsatian
pricks his ears

We take a trip to a small fishing village named Horcón and stop for a while to look at the pelicans there. The fishermen have the local pelican population completely spoilt. They are so lazy that they literally queue up to be fed their fish along the edge of the quayside. The pelicans don't even bother fishing for themselves anymore. In fact, some of them are so fat they can barely waddle. San Pedro, the patron saint of fishermen, watches over it all, grimacing from a rocky perch out in the bay. Put the Herrenvolk in charge of Chile and those pelicans will be whipped into shape I'm telling you!

flea-market in Valparaiso
a German helmet
eaten by rust

A strange brew… On we travel ... next thing we smell horse manure. "That's the smell of mushrooms," says Jochen. A Chinese man has a factory here employing about 200 workers.

"That smell reminds me of something that happened when I was in the Andes. A group of us were travelling through the mountains when our guide was struck down with a sickness. I had no medicine to give him and the poor man was vomiting constantly. A terrible dose of vomiting and diarrhoea. We were very far from home and there was no easy or obvious solution to our predicament. Anyway, our guide was in a bad way, so sick that he was getting desperate. He asked me to get him a piece of horse manure. He swallowed it down and the next morning he was as healthy as a trout!"

On this route are many pilgrims. Tomorrow is the eighth of December—and the people will travel the final kilometre of their pilgrimage walking on their knees as a penance. At the end of their walk, they will kiss a statue of the Virgin Mary, the Virgén de los Vasques.

Planxty of the Parrots...A shopping centre in Viña del Mar. A small boy is staring at a window. Yes? And? He is whistling. And? The music! The sound he makes is the music of the rainforest, a type of whistling sound the like of which I have never heard before. It is the rhythm of a strange place, the rhythm of the otherworld; to my ears it comes from an Urwald, a place where no human being has been, somewhere on the edge of the world. His music a planxty of parrots.
We pay a visit to Pablo Neruda's house in Valparaiso, a house which is now an eccentric museum. Who else but Neruda could
compose an ode to a tomato!

The street
filled up with tomatoes,
noon,
summer,
light is
halved
like
a
tomato,
its juice
runs
through the streets.
In December,
unabated,
the tomato
invades
the kitchen,
it enters at lunchtime,
takes
its ease

on countertops,
among glasses,
butter dishes,
blue saltcellars.
It sheds
its own light,
benign majesty.
Unfortunately, we must
murder it:
the knife
sinks
into living flesh,
red
viscera
a cool
sun,
profound,
inexhaustible,
populates the salads
of Chile….

If you don't know it, read the whole poem. It's mouth-watering.

A Big Mystery... We have to stop in Lima, Peru, before landing at Los Angeles Airport. I take a look out of the window of the plane and it's just as well that I do—let me tell you. I had completely forgotten that we would be passing over one of the most spectacular sights in the world. How come the pilot doesn't make an announcement about it? Is he asleep or what? Maybe he did announce it and I was dozing at the time. The sight below us would knock a bishop for six! I'm referring of course to the Nazca Lines in the Andes, proof—if Erich von Däniken's theory is correct—that a secret airport or motorway was once built here for alien visitors. Doubt it but, yes, you have to rub your eyes when looking down at those lines from a height.

The lines cutting across the landscape may be very long but it is not easy to make out their patterns at first glance. Besides the straight lines (that would indeed remind you of a secret highway of sorts), there are many other mysterious patterns here which are not easy to decipher. Some of them appear to be in the shape of birds while others look like spiders, plants or monkeys. And—more amazing still—in the middle of this great desert is the shape of a great whale.

The Nazca tribe in southern Peru were the creators of these patterns although they never really had the opportunity to view their handiwork in its completeness. It is only with the arrival of the aeroplane that the incredible beauty of these patterns can be truly appreciated. And talk of mystery! It was Maria Reiche who escaped from Germany in 1939 who first studied these patterns. She was a mathematician by trade and it was her great ambition in life to try to decipher the riddle of these patterns. What are they? By the 1970s, scientists were beginning to undertake more sophisticated studies of these patterns with the help of computers. One theory put forward to explain the Nazca Lines is that they are the paths once followed by pilgrims, paths carved out as they followed ancient river-beds and streams. Who know?

The Disembodied Eye ... Did the Nazca people ever get the opportunity to see their handiwork from high up in the firmament, I ask myself? I'm not suggesting that that they had flying balloons which soared high over the mountain peaks or anything. But what about the shamans or seers, people who could eat a particular mushroom or herb, something which gave them another eye on the world, another door to perception? In this context, it is worth looking at what Gordon Wasson, an American banker and the first person (that I know of) who described the practice of eating magic mushrroms in Southern Mexico (1957):

> ...the visions came whether our eyes were opened or closed. They were vivid in colour, always harmonious. They began with art motifs, angular such as might decorate carpets of textiles or wallpaper or the drawing board of an architect...
>
> (Shamans Through Time)

Isn't this the same sight that I see down below me now as I sit here in this aeroplane. One more sentence from Wasson to round off my theoretical proposition? "There I was poised in space, a disembodied eye, invisible, incorporeal, seeing but not seen..."(ibid).

One way or the other, I am really happy that no clouds came between us and the incredible sight that is the Nazca Lines. The view lasted for no more than three minutes, but the sight of whatever it was will stay with me for a long time.

A Long Sentence...

"I travelled around the world recently and I didn't think much of it," Thomas Beecham once wrote. Did he ever get to see Southern Peru, I wonder? We're on the wander again…by plane this time. From Santiago to Lima and from Lima to Los Angeles, and from the City of Angels to San Diego, California, where Eithne's uncle, Hugo, lives. He's a Maguire from County Monaghan who set out for the New World more than fifty years ago. He has a house on the hill, a swimming pool in the garden and a horde of hummingbirds as regular visitors, punctual and as bold as the navy jet fighters which pass overhead from morning till night. They'd swipe a rib of hair from your head, they're so cheeky, these same hummingbirds. We have travelled a long way now and our journey is nearing its end.

Bad Taste in My Mouth …Prior to landing in San Diego, we were all handed sweets that go by the strange name of Trident Advantage. These pills are supposed to help strengthen the teeth and ease the breathing as the plane loses altitude on its descent. I check the Trident Advantage packet a few times—just to make sure that we hadn't been given something else by mistake –detergent tablets or some such thing!

The bright lights of Mexico wink at us from across the same bay that is home to a fleet of threatening warships. Each and every house has its American flag flying proudly outside. We head out for a walk and pass a person in a wheelchair. Even he has his own small version of the Stars and Stripes flag attached to his wheelchair; it flutters hopefully in the breeze. There's a fat guy sitting in the park, a man by the name of Skip. He is reading Tarot cards but nobody seems interested. (Maybe it was in the cards that he'd have no customers today). He has been reading Tarot cards for thirty years, he says. I feel sorry for Skip and let him do a reading for me. The cards indicate that I am repressing my ego, Skip tells me. If I wasn't suppressing this aspect of my personality I could achieve a great deal more in my life.

"You need to start a war, Gabriel! You need to get in there, into the heat of battle. It's a war, man! That's what the cards say. And another thing, the cards say that you will win!"

I knew it! War madness in the air. That's what George Harrison says on the Nonduality Magazine video clip, the world is being run by raving lunatics.

I am tempted to choke poor Skip while simultaneously informing him that I am sick to death of wars. Skip gives me a small present when as we say goodbye. A bottle of bubbles!

"Go and blow some bubbles in the park, Gabriel! Let it all go man!"

"I'll definitely do that, Skip! Thanks very much!"

He obviously has me down for a softie…a bit of an idiot. A loser.

The shopping malls are like giant cathedrals and it is reported that (subsequent to the September the eleventh attacks) the sales of military or soldier-type toys went through the roof.

How can it be stopped? Should an attempt be made to assassinate Santa Claus? Is this the war that those Tarot cards were really referring to? Imagine a Fox News announcer:

> And the war on terrorism took a bizarre twist today: in San Diego, an obscure, minor Irish poet, Gay Rosenblatt—believed to be associated with al-Qaeda—used an American flag to strangle Santa Claus. Before Mr. Rosenblatt could make his escape, the Irish terrorist and a female accomplice, believed to be his wife, were gunned down by angry school children.

Speaking of George Harrison, The Economist has an obituary with no reference whatsoever to the man's religious beliefs. Why can't they just say it out straight. They believe in one god and one god only—all-powerful Mammon.

A Return Visit to Kerala

A year later and we are back in southern India and it is a salutary thing to be able to read The Hindu newspaper again. I missed it! The advertisements are brilliant, especially the tiny ads inserted by astrologers. I see one here from somebody who requests that you send him your thumbprint—yes an impression of your thumb—which he will then use to give you an astrological reading, and all for the small price of fifty cents. He will consult the Agasthiya Maharshie, an ancient text written on palm leaves, and tell you what kind of a person you were when you were first born, various pieces of valuable knowledge about your parents (things that you never knew yourself, maybe), the diseases you are afflicted with (unknown to you) or the future diseases that will afflict you; he will also discuss a range of other issues relating to marital matters, business, travel, politics and the enemies you have (the latter, also unknown to you!). Where would you could get a better deal than that? By the way, if you're a woman, the astrologer requires an imprint of your left thumb, if a man it's the right thumb. A load of old mumbo-jumbo? Don't knock it.

We have returned to Kerala to visit the city's waterways and lagoons. Now we have time to explore them properly. We have brought binoculars with us also in order to spot the many varieties of birds living on the water. Looking out the window in Cochin (Kochi) what do I see? "One boat east and one boat west"—as the Aran Islander once said. The city of Cochin is built on a series of islands. And what do I hear? The same rogues we heard last year. Those noisy crows.

The Taj Malabar hotel has a sign hanging high on the wall—"Do not feed the crows!". They are well-fed already. There is heavy rain in the sky and clouds as big as Ireland. What matter. We are back in Kerala anyway. It took us four hours to drive from Trivandrum to Cochin. Signposts along the way advising motorists to drive with caution:

HURRY BRINGS WORRY
SPEED THRILLS—BUT KILLS
RUSH MEANS CRUSH

The local corporation has a poet on its books by the looks of it. We visit the docks which are a hive of activity. Goods ships, passenger vessels, fishing boats from Sri Lanka which have been pounded by the police.

A Civilization in Decline…A few minutes of peace in the synagogue. We had to remove our shoes at the entrance, an example of the influence Hinduism has had on the Jewish culture of Cochin. A group of visitors arrive at the synagogue just after us. They are Hindus mainly—"Where is the idol?" one woman asks? "Where is their god?" The guide showing them around looks carefully at the questioner and puts his finger to his head. "Their god is in the mind," he says, a response which leaves the woman with a bewildered look on her face.

The Jews of Kerala suffered persecution from the Portuguese, this despite the fact that they helped the explorers a good deal, working with them as translators, astrologers and traders etc. The Dutch and the English, both of whom were Protestant peoples and who came after the Portuguese, treated the Jews even better and tension between the Jews and the native princes proved a rarity. In the 1940s there were about 2500 Jews living in Kerala. The foundation of the state of Israel signalled the death-knell for the Jews of India, however, as many of them decided to return to the Holy Land from which they had been exiled for 2000 years.

Any writer who happens to visit Cochin will enjoy the sight of the following signpost: HONEST PEN HOSPITAL! In this place, you can get your pen fixed on the spot—so that you can get back to your writing again as good as ever!

The dance of the gods…Another reason we were eager to revisit Kerala was because we were keen to see the theatrical dance known as Kathakali. Old-style singing, frenetic drumming and mime, all in the form of stylized dance. In the visitor's book we write that the ancient and living tradition that is Kathakali is a more valuable Indian institution than the Taj Mahal itself. One of the local tour organisers glances at what I have written and a look of genuine pride suffuses his face. You don't see that kind of satisfaction being expressed in the West. We're all wise-guys now!

We are allowed into the dressing rooms to watch the preparations for the dance. The actors apply their make-up to one another, one man on his back, while another male actor applies the make-up to his face. Nobody takes any notice of the time (there is no clock visible anywhere) and the actors are unperturbed whether there is a "full house" or not. Ultimately, the Kathakali (the emphasis is on the second syllable of the word)—is a ritual performed between the dancers and the gods. The audience are just witnesses to the performance of the ritual. The make-up man is both deaf and dumb as it happens and he replies to a couple of questions by wetting his finger and inscribing some mysterious signs on the floor.

The meaning of the play is explained to us. Angels and devils is its theme; what else? Normally this dance-drama begins at ten o'clock at night and continues on until dawn. Or, as with the Irish Fiannaíocht tales of old, the story or play can continue for a number of nights. As it turned out we tourists (barbarians) only saw a shortened version of the play.

The make-up and the costumes were extremely impressive and it was very evident how seriously the actors approached their craft. One can easily see how this dramatic art form would have had such a huge effect on the communities of rural villages in the recent past. Rural audiences of previous decades would have been transfixed at the sight of the Kathakali—that much is certain. The audience would resolve thereafter to be very well-behaved—afraid to get involved in any devilment—until the next time the travelling theatre troupe came around. Even the sound of the drum—the sudda mandalam—is so elemental and fierce, it would put the heart crossways in you.

One of the actors was a man playing the part of a woman, He was incredibly realistic, so much so that you'd have sworn he actually was a woman—the way he fed a baby at the breast. The hands and the eyes are used a great deal in the Kathakali in order to narrate the story; it is the cosmic feminine which always wins the day in these dramas. This is entirely natural given that the Kathakali genre is based on goddess worship. Sooner or later, we will have to engage once more with the feminine virtues, to bring some more yin into the world; if not, then the forces of unbridled gung-ho, the yang of warmongers, will destroy whatever is left of the planet. ('Gung-ho' was once a lovely Chinese word, gōnghé, meaning 'to work together', before the Marines took it over!)

A puja ceremony honouring the goddesses is being performed in a New Age art gallery here in Cochin, a gallery which doubles as a café. I ask the owner why somebody has left a pen on the altar. It has been placed in front of the statue of Sarasvati, the patron of artists. The gallery owner tells me that he wants to be a writer someday and it was he who placed the pen there. I notice a photograph of an Indian woman in amongst the holy pictures.

"Who is she?"

"That my mother," he says. "She died ten years ago." I am very touched by this gesture of his—his mother with her own place here amongst the goddesses —individual and cosmic reverence all in one. Is it any wonder that I am so fond of the people of Kerala? We should all renew our understanding of the value of life itself, respect for holy Mother Earth, the power of the living feminine, shakti, the power of birth and rebirth.

The Kubjika Tantra says: 'Whosever has seen the feet of a woman, let him worship them as those of his guru.' Amen to that.

That man who was remembering his mother amongst the pantheon of goddesses, he was really honouring every mother that ever walked the earth. I was moved to write a poem:

Táim ag dul as radharc ionat
Mar is gnách, mar is dual dom.
A Mháthair!
Bainne na Bó Finne
Sceitheann ina chaise cheolmhar
As do chíoch chlé
Ar mo theanga, im scornach
Is ar fud m'inní.
Is tú m'aonchothú anois
Is go brách
Gan teimheal díom aon áit

Ach ionatsa.
Do bharróg is docht dochuimsithe
Do ghuth! Nach séimh,
Á! Sarasvati!
OM!

I am disappearing
As usual, as is my nature,
In You, Mother.
The Milk of the White Cow
Comes cascading melodiously
From your left breast
On my tongue, in my throat,
In all my vital organs.
Your are my only nourishment now
And forever.
Nowhere am I
But in You.
Your strong, immeasurable embrace,
Your voice! How gentle,
Ah, Sarasvati!
OM!

Life and Death…the water hyacinth only grows in fresh water. I see it now as it drifts with the tide, driving onwards…towards its death. Plants scattered as on a chessboard moving, growing and then dying away again...life…failure…life and death in that eternal erotic struggle.

Land of the Little People…We are in an engine-propelled boat on our way to a quarter of Kerala known—in the local language –

as Kuttanad, land of the little people. No, dwarves they are not, nor fairies. The area is thus called because the inhabitants were seen to be habitually up to their knees in rice paddies.

Would we like to visit a farm? Certainly. Off we go to the Philipkutty farm in Kumarakom in the middle of Lake Vembanad. It's mostly a spice farm, land reclaimed by the grandfather of the woman of the house. Here are figs, bananas, pineapples, papaya, ginger, turmeric, jackfruit (we've never seen such a whopper). We catch them at various stages of growth and marvel at the cinnamon which we realize is bark. And pepper is a vine. We are on a 50 acre farm on an island that didn't exist a hundred years ago.

We buy some nutmeg and pepper and remind ourselves how spices attracted the early explorers, not as condiments but as ways to preserve food. Turmeric is highly prized medicinally, good for liver, heart, skin, eyes, prostrate, and more, so say the Ayurvedic texts.

For anybody looking to spend a quiet week away from the noisy fever of life—in a place surrounded by glens and lakes, canals and lagoons, a place where the kingfisher sits patiently on a branch awaiting its moment of glory—then they would do well to spend some time in a place as serene as this farm, set amongst the coconut trees.

Free drink …Coconuts sold in Irish shops are all fuzzy and hard. They are very different here. In Kerala they are smooth and bald and the juice within is as sweet as the milk you would feed a baby. There is nothing better than this coconut milk to staunch your thirst and many is the time that we stopped on the side of the street for a quick swig from a roadside coconut vendor. Cans or bottles aren't required here; you simply insert a straw into the top of the coconut and drink your fill. The Coca-Cola people can't be too happy with the god who presented this free drink to the people of Kerala.

Let us bow... We're going to do some more travelling on the smaller waterways of Kerala, this time in a traditional house-boat. The kettuvallam was once a barge for transporting rice. Eithne accidentally strikes her head off the door of the barge and we gather around to check that she is OK. We rub her head for a while and she comes to herself again. The entrances to these traditional barges were always deliberately constructed low to the ground. This was because people needed to bow before entering the boat and thus show their respect willy-nilly.

Mazes... Through and along a maze of lakes, rivers and canals we sail; each time we reach masses of water hyacinths, small islands of them—the barge-man uses his barge-pole to prevent us becoming trapped in them. We pass children on the banks and their mantra is the following: Pen! Schoolpen! Unfortunately, the only pen I have with me is the one with which I am writing this diary. A water-snake swims close by, close enough to offer us his blessing. The coconut trees decorate both sides of the canal, every tree equal in height. There must be millions of coconut trees here. Kerala alone produces 8,000,000,000 coconuts annually – pity the poor devil whose job it is to count them all!

The coconut has countless uses; it serves as fuel for the fire and as roofing for the house; it is used as a post or a marker; handicrafts are carved from the wood; the coconut leaves are used for thatching and brush-making; the copra is used for the production of oil and the baking of cakes; the coconut husk is used for ropes and mats and the coconut juice for the refining of brown sugar and alcohol. Interestingly, we don't see even one drunkard throughout the entire time we spend in Kerala.

Letter from the Gulf....The "letter from America" kept many families alive in Ireland. The people of Kerala anxiously await similar letters; the only difference is that their letters come from the United Arab Emirates.

Ocean of Light... Night is falling. We light the citrus candles which keep the insects away. We open a bottle of wine. In the water the shadows dance an ancient waltz and the music of nature reminds us that the darkness of night is just a temporary aberration and the world will soon bathe again in an ocean of light.

an egret stands in a lagoon
on the flagstones
sound of washed clothes

I have a bad night on that barge—between the heat, mosquitoes and the incessant crowing of the cockerels—and there is another sound...a sound like rolling thunder. If it's not the sky rumbling, it must be the sound of vedi vashipadu—the ritual of explosions, a tradition which makes a bigger racket than thunder ever would.

A visit next morning to Saint Mary's Cathedral, the Syrian Catholic Cathedral of Cheripally. The dead are kept in the graveyard here for three or four years before their bones are transferred to the ossuary so that room can be made for the next batch of dead people. The bones in the ossuary are burnt each time it becomes full. The walls of the church are decorated with wall hangings made from plants. Characters from the Old Testament for the most part, Noah to the fore One can understand how people who live and work on water would have a special empathy with the honest soul that was Noah.

Christianity has become over-Westernised, repulsively so in some of its fundamentalist forms. I think of Henri le Saux, the Benedictine monk from Brittany, who ended up near the holy mountain of Arunachala in India and becomes Swami Abhishiktananda, whose central belief was as follows:

> 'Man's primary task is to penetrate within and there discover himself. Whoever has not found himself within himself has not yet found God; and whoever has not found God within himself has not yet found himself…'

Quack-quack! There are boats out in the water here which are very similar to the Irish naomhóg or curragh. They are collecting shellfish. Once opened, the shells are used to make cement. A boat passes us, full of clay pots. And who's this bucko who's heading in our direction now? Duck salesman! chirps a member of the crew who hasn't spoken a word until now. No doubt about it, they're all out today. In the river there are men standing, up to their waists in water, washing themselves and shaving. On the canal bank, a group of boys relax quietly, their fishing rods tipping the surface of the water. If paradise exists, then it must be a water paradise rather than a paradise of air. The souls of the just eddying and flowing from place to place, rippling out into eternity. And there will be no mosquitoes allowed into this Heaven—not into the seventh heaven anyway.

We say our goodbyes to the boatmen. Before we leave we're asked to fill out a questionnaire, rating the boat trip. The food? Excellent. And so on. Any suggestions to make the journey even more pleasant? Yes. Train an army of crows to hunt down the mosquitoes; hunt them and eat them all warm and fresh. Who knows? Maybe the local corporation will take the suggestion on board?

Maybe it will be subject to intense debate in the halls of local government. Who can tell? If this recommendation finds acceptance, the corporation's poet will have a new job on the marketing side of things:

Maybe he go
With help of the crow?

Our driver is waiting for us. We've a bit of a journey ahead, uphill to the higher reaches of Kerala, an area that borders Tamil Nadu. This is the territory of the tiger—there is still the odd one left here, the occasional descendant of those few which weren't shot by the British during the era of the Raj. The driver of the car is a Christian, married to a Hindu. Neither family has spoken to one another for the past twenty years—and it doesn't look like they will anytime soon either. The guidebook for tourists claims that all religious groups in Kerala live in perfect harmony with one another; the reality is clearly a bit different, however. There are religious and ethnic tensions simmering beneath the surface although they are not half as obvious here as they are in other parts of India.

We've reached Thekaddy . I thought the place would be at too high an altitude, the air too cool—that it would be too far away from the waterways for the mosquitoes to live here. I was wrong! They're here too, those pesky little monsters. I wake during the night to spray more anti-mosquito repellent on myself and to put on a long-sleeved shirt. Eithne sprinkles lemongrass oil on the four corners of the bed, not unlike somebody blessing the bed with holy water in days of yore. Still, the mosquitoes keep coming. Our next resort is prayer. What saint would hear our plea? Listen here, didn't Saint Colm have a fly as his pet? Right so. Here we go.

A Naomh Colm Cille a raibh peata cuileoige agat
Cosain sinnn, impímid ort, ar na diabhail bheaga go léir
Mo chreach is mo chás!
Atá ag teacht idir sinn agus codladh na hoíche.
Múin míneas dóibh agus béasa
Agus tabhair slán sinn as ucht Dé

Sinne agus gach neach eile atá i bpéin anocht in Thekaddy, Áiméan.

St. Columba, you who had a pet fly
Protect us we implore you from all wee devils
Oh woe and desolation!
That come between us and a night's sleep.
Teach them gentleness and manners
And bring us out of harm's way in the name of God
We and everyone else in pain tonight in Thekaddy, Amen.

It worked!

This time last year I was reading R.K. Narayan. At the moment I am reading extracts from Indian Thought edited by the same man. Indian Thought was a philosophy journal which lasted for just four issues. Here's an extract from a letter Professor Quentin-Anderson sent Narayan's father:

> Why do you always think in mortal terms? The dying deserve gratitude and envy. They do not desire our pity. You have a million years in which to strive to become what your mother would have you to be where the soul sits free and all the noble mothers await us to lead us into God's garden where the eternal children foregather far from the shady sadness of the world we must outgrow...

Those sentiments lift my heart. Sursum corda!

We leave the invigorating air of Thekkady behind. The tiger did not make an appearance...and we hit the road again. A five-hour drive south towards the seaside town of Varkala. An Ayurvedic doctor gives us a powder called eladi choornam for the relief of mosquito stings. The potion has to be mixed with a small amount of water before it can be applied as a paste. The paste is applied to the mosquito bites for an hour and then removed. It's a fairly time-consuming process—particularly if you are in a hurry. After you are finished with the paste you need to apply a particular oil to the bite. This oil known as nalpamardi thailam is an oil which is prepared in accordance with a special formula as prescribed in the text known as Sahasrayogam. I apply the relevant paste and oil but Eithne shouts out—"You're turning yellow!" I walk over to a mirror. Sure enough. I'm more Chinese-looking than a Chinaman!

"I'm not sure about this crack..." Eithne says.

"Will I sprinkle a drop or two of oil on you?" I ask.

"Keep that damned stuff away from me," exclaims the snowy-breasted pearl. Later on, when she sees how effective the stuff is, Eithne changes her mind. There isn't a mark or a bite left on me—it is amazing. Eithne decides to follow the same ritual as I did—long-drawn out though it may be.

A death notice...We check the email. There is a message to say that my father has died. He passed away on the island of Naxos, in Greece.

Scéala báis…
ialtóg torthaí ar crochadh
fá shuan

news of a death...
the fruitbat suspened
in slumber

It would be difficult to celebrate my father's life and death here in Varkala, a place where the life force bursts forth from every frond and branch, every bush and shrub. A few drinks in his honour? The only alcohol available here is a pale (Indian) imitation of Scottish whiskey—a brand with a touristy name, Bagpipe or something similar. That would never do. We'll have some kind of a wake for him when we get back to Ireland.

In the meantime, we head southwards to Sri Lanka and one of the greatest holy relics in the world (or not!). That's if it is still there and the Portuguese didn't bring it with them to Goa years ago and burn it there, as some people believe—Buddha's tooth.

The End

AFTERWORD

Professor Michael Cronin
(Dublin City University, Ireland)

When one goes in search of the "other" place, it is often that one finds a reflection of home. In actual fact, it is the sign of a worthwhile journey when such a mirror of self and home presents itself. From the odyssey of Ulysees to Chatwin's pilgrimage in Australia, not only do travellers encounter that which is strange or new; the "other", that is new peoples, cultures and languages; travellers must also negotiate the "other" within themselves. In many respects, a travel book is a journey into the inner world, the interior of the human being...the soul. And each wanderer is alone...following his own path; every trace and trail is individual...unique. In the end it is the journey to the interior which concerns us most of all, not the final destination. The path to understanding is strewn with rocks and thistles but no matter. While the final goal may remain obscured or occluded; it is the journey itself which reveals the lines on the map, the contours of that thing which may never reveal itself. Gabriel Rosenstock has written a travel memoir which is thoughtful and perceptive. Not for him the bare bones of the official guidebooks nor the sanitized and lifeless rhetoric of the official tourist trail. No. Rosenstock endeavours to capture the moment behind the moment, the revelation that lies like a trace just behind the mundane facts of human intercourse...of living. He digs beneath each tree and rock until he reaches the source, the sap which rises up in the deeper moments, the meaning which underscores the vestige of the living word. Not only does he do his utmost to explain the foreignness of the Indian and Japanese worlds to us, the beauty and richness of these very diverse cultures, the familiar in the strange. Rosenstock also employs the travel writing genre to provide an insight into his own spirituality and his view of the world, his own artistic sensibility. Not for

Rosenstock the flights of fancy which characterise some philosophers of the human heart. He visits real people in scattered corners of the world. He warns us of the problems we generate for ourselves as human beings when we refuse to engage with other races and cultures or when we dimiss those peoples deemed to inhabit the world's fringes. A good deal of this travel account was written while the world was once again inhaling the vicious breath of war; there was an urgency and an immediacy to Rosenstock's elucidation of the human values that are peace and the usurpation of stereotype. The cultural dismissal of other peoples and cultures that has given rise to centuries of historical suspicion and enmity is as characteristic of modernity as it is was of the ancient world. Again and again, during the course of this book Rosenstock criticizes the lazy look or the unquestioning glance, the assumption of a perennial conflict between East and West. Rosenstock regularly reminds us of cultural links which are more ancient than the desert and which link the Eastern and Western spiritual and aesthetic traditions; Ireland's hagiographic tradition and the hagiographic traditions of India, for example; the animism of Japan and that which permeates the Gaelic tradition.

Of course the travel writer is obliged to describe the cultural tenets and attitudes which divide the "foreign" culture from that with which the writer is more familiar. There is an attendant duty to illuminate the congruencies which exist between the familiar and the exotic, however—and Rosenstock is more alert to these than many travel writers who have preceded him. Arguably, this latter responsibility has never been more grave than at this current juncture in world history, when one set of ideologies and values seeks to impose itself—whether politically or militarily on others. Travel writing and history are subjects which have not often been dealt with together within the realm of Irish language literary criticism. This is a lacuna which is difficult to understand when one considers that rich and lively tradition which spans the early writings of the invasions to more recent travel accounts including: Turas go Páras (Journey to Paris) - Liam Ó Rinn, Seal ag Ródaíocht (Wandering Awhile)—Proinsias Mac Maghnais, Siúlach Scéalach (The Person who Travels has many Stories) - Eibhlín Ní Mhurchú. Súil

Timpeall (A Walk Around) - Séamus Ó Néill, Manchán ar Seachrán (Manchán on the Wander) - Manchán Magan and Rince ar na Ballaí (Dancing on the Walls)—Dermot Somers. It is no surprise either that documentaries exploring travelling and travel writing have proved so popular on TG4. The educated storyteller and chronicler, the travel guide who provides a new window on the majesty of the world, has always had a great following amongst the Gaels. Gabriel Rosenstock's chronicle is a valuable addition to this living tradition in the Irish language. Whether Rosenstock is journeying between Dublin and India or between Sydney and San Diego, the reader is always aware that he/she is in the company of not only a seasoned traveller but one who shortens the road with story and anecdote. Visiting India and Japan Rosenstock meets other writers, thereby proferring us readers with vivid and unusual insights into the cultural life of these countries, both antiquarian and artistic. A noted polyglot and Irish-language writer, it is no surprise that Rosenstock pays particular attention to the linguistic terrains he encounters including efforts by other linguistic minorities to preserve what they have in the face of a seemingly relentless tide of cultural homogeneity, the tyranny of the same.

Unlike many of his contemporaries who invariably use one of the world's "major" languages as their written medium, Rosenstock pays due attention to the importance played in the promulgation of identity and the defining of borders between the local and the outsider. Without displaying such sensitivities, it is only possible for any travel writer to gain but a partial understanding of any people or culture. Mindful of this reality, Gabriel and his wife Eithne make a conscious effort to learn (and use) some of the local language as spoken by the people of Kerala, India.

Rosenstock's observation with respect to language use is supported by our experiences here in the West where the statistics clearly indicate that the number of Westerners who learn foreign languages—(they are also the group who travel the most, incidentally, given that they have the material means to do so)—are, as with the foreigners in Kerala, still small in numbers. It is observations such as this which make Gabriel Rosenstock's travel diary all the more valuable as a social document. The modern world may provide incredible opportunities for travel and the movement of people, but migration and respect for cultural differences are not always one and the same thing. In a way, Rosenstock's art bears more similarities with the travel writings of the honnete home, of the eighteenth century, than it does with some of his modern-day contemporaries. His aesthetic is a journey that is intellectual, literary, but above all, spiritual. Rosenstock is able to capture the unique spirit of each and every new destination in a manner that is accurate, yet complex. This is because he has already visited this "other" place beforehand in his mind. Like any good traveller he has already prepared himself for the journey. He has informed himself about his new port of call and knows its scents and colours. His prior reading serves to confirm many of the impressions which were already intimated to him This immediacy places his writing on a much richer plane than the bare sketches and summaries which characterise many travel guides of the present-day. In addition to this, Rosenstock is a sharp observer of human nature; a writer who positively rails against those cynical or arrogant attitudes which once characterised the touring Westerner of old. Put simply, Rosenstock endeavours to see the world through the eyes of his hosts; he puts on their shoes and walks in their traces. Rosenstock is also the most postmodern of travel writers. The text of Ólann mo Mhiúil as an nGainséis is dotted with links to useful websites and addresses so that the reader can continue on with their journey and follow different virtual pathways even after they have finished reading the book. Not for the first time, Rosenstock has shaken things up; he has given a new "literary turn" to the Irish language once again.

Island people are not noted for their sedate natures. The perennial searchings and imaginings of other places is an essential aspect of their existence. Again and again, they subvert the proposition that to be an islander is to be narrow in outlook or perspective. It is the opposite that is true, in fact. A reality which is clear to anyone who undertakes even a brief review of Irish-language travel accounts from the earliest times. Gabriel Rosenstock alludes to these early travellers in his account too; he draws from the same well of tradition. Those early Irish monks for whom the navigation was both an eager quest for learning and a form of spiritual enlightenment. Rosenstock reminds us that the energy and vision of our forebears has never been more in need of resurgence than it is in the Ireland of today. "Travel broadens the mind," they say. It also serves as a rich reminder of what we have at home. The necessity to preserve our own cultural and philosophical inheritance. The preservation and development of what we still have becomes more urgent when we encounter other traditions, other cultures, other ways of seeing the beauty of a changing world anew. All of the world's major religions make clear that our lives are journeys. A poignant reminder of this fact occurs near the end of Rosenstock's narrative when, having arrived back in Kerala, he receives news of his father's death. Rosenstock has reached one destination at the same time as has his father—thousands of miles away on an island in Greece. Another essential tenet of all religions and all philosophies is the principle that it is the journey which matters infinitely more than does the destination. As we come to the end of another long journey—the literary treat which Rosenstock has served up here—it is clear that we have travelled the road in the company of a soul-mate whose insights are as perceptive as they are joyous, a traveller who has the gift of feeling. Having read this travel account we are prepared to set out on our most arduous journey yet, the journey towards self-understanding.

(SELECT) GLOSSARY

Joseph Rudyard Kipling

Joseph Rudyard Kipling (1865-1936) was an English poet, short-story writer, and novelist chiefly remembered for his celebration of British imperialism, his tales and poems relating to the lives of British soldiers in India, his children's stories. Kipling was one of the most popular writers in England, in both prose and verse, in the late 19th and early 20th centuries. He is best known today for his works of fiction, including *Kim* (1901) (a tale of adventure) and his many short stories. He is also highly-regarded for his poetry, amongst them, the collection *If* (1910). Kipling received the 1907 Nobel Prize for Literature.

Heinrich Schütz

Heinrich Schütz (1585-1672) was a highly-regarded German composer and organist. Monteverdi and he are often considered to be amongst the most important composers of the seventeenth century He wrote what is thought to be the first German opera, *Dafne*, initially performed at Torgau in 1627. Unfortunately, the music composed for this opera was lost at a later date and has never been found. He is commemorated as a musician in the Calendar of Saints of the Lutheran Church, along with both Bach and Handel.

"The Fields of Athenry"

"The Fields of Athenry" is an Irish folk ballad set during the Great Irish Famine (1845-1848) about a fictional man named Michael who is said to have been from Athenry in County Galway. The song describes how this man Michael had been sentenced to "transportation" to Botany Bay, Australia, because he had stolen food for his starving family. It is a widely known and popular anthem as song at many Irish sporting events. A version of this song with the title amended to "The

Fields of Anfield" is frequently sung by Liverpool football supporters at their matches.

Dhow

A dhow is the generic name for a number of traditional sailing boats as used in the Red Sea and the Indian Ocean region. Some historians believe the dhow was invented by the Arabs but this is disputed by some others. Today, the dhow is still primarily used as a trading vessel and to carry heavy items such as fruit, fresh water or other merchandise along the coasts of the Arabian Peninsula, Pakistan, India, Bangladesh and in parts of East Africa.

V. S. Naipaul

Born in 1932, Vidiadhar Surajprasad "V. S." Naipaul is a much-celebrated Indo-Trinidadian-British writer who is known for his novels focusing on the legacy of the British Empire and British colonialism. He has also written travel writing and essays. In 2001, he was awarded the Nobel Prize for Literature.

Bhakti poetry

Some scholars divide Hindi literature divided into four prominent genres or styles—i.e. Bhakti (devotional poetry) Shringar (poetry as associated with beauty), Veer-Gatha (heroic praise-poetry extolling the deeds of brave warriors) and Adhunik (modern forms of poetry). Each of these forms, bhakti poetry included, encompass literature as written in the various Hindi languages, languages which themselves include a diversity of written forms.

Svengali

The word "svengali", has come to mean a person who, with evil intent, controls another person by persuasion or deceit. The Svengali may use apparent kindness or other forms of manipulation to ensure that they gain "control" over the other person.

Haiku

Traditionally, haiku is a form of Japanese lyric poetry, as written in three unrhymed lines of five, seven, and five syllables. Although haiku-writing has assumed different forms as written by Western writers, it traditionally involves the exploration or invocation of some aspect of nature and the seasons.

Ayurvedic

Ayurveda or ayurvedic medicine is a system of traditional medicine native to India. In Sanskrit, the word āyus, implies "longevity", while veda, means "knowledge" or "science". Over the centuries ayurvedic practitioners have developed a range of medicinal preparations and surgical procedures for the treatment of many ailments. In the western world today, many practices derived from Ayurvedic medicine are often considered a form of complementary or alternative medicine

Krishna

Krishna is an important figure in Hinduism and is traditionally attributed the authorship of the *Bhagavad Gita,* (the Song of God), a 700-verse Hindu scripture that is part of the ancient Sanskrit epic, the *Mahabharata.* He is known as the eighth and "complete" avatar of Lord Vishnu who has come on earth to restore Dharma in a time of great dharmic imbalance. Krishna is identified as an historical individual who participated in the events of the *Mahabharata.*

Manannán

Manannán mac Lir is the "God of the Sea" in Irish mythology. He is strongly linked with aspects of the Otherworld, the weather and the mists between the worlds. Manannán is a character who appears widely in Irish literature, in addition to Scottish and Manx legend. He is cognate with the Welsh figure Manawydan fab Llŷr.

Tagore

Poet and translator, Rabindranath Tagore (1861-1941) was a Bengali polymath who reshaped his region's literature and music. Author of the widely-celebrated collection of devotional song-poems known as the *Gitanjali* he became the first non-European Nobel prize-winner when he was awarded the prestigious literary prize in 1913

Chesterton

G.K. (Gilbert Keith) Chesterton (1874-1936) was an English writer whose output was incredibly prolific and diverse. His writings included philosophy, ontology, poetry, plays, journalism, public lectures and debates, literary and art criticism, biography, Christian apologetics, and fiction, including fantasy and detective fiction. Today, Chesterton particularly celebrated for his reasoned "apologetics" and even some of his staunchest critics have admired the evident breadth of knowledge and universal appeal of such works as *Orthodoxy* (1908) *and The Everlasting Man* (1925). As a political thinker, Chesterton was a critic of both progressivism and conservatism.

Author:

Gabriel Rosenstock is a poet and haikuist, author/translator of over 150 books, mostly in Irish (Gaelic). A member of Aosdána (the Irish Academy of arts and letters), he taught haiku at the Schule für Dichtung (Poetry Academy) in Vienna and has given readings in Europe, North, South and Central America, Australia, India and Japan. A former Chairman of Poetry Ireland/Éigse Éireann, he is an Honorary Life Member of the Irish Translators' and Interpreters' Association and a Founding Associate of The Haiku Foundation. Salmon Poetry published his debut volume in English in 2009, *Uttering Her Name* and in the same year Cambridge Scholars Publishing (UK) brought out his twin-volume reflections on haiku, *Haiku Enlightenment* and *Haiku, the Gentle Art of Disappearing*.

Translator:

Dr. Mícheál Ó hAodha lectures in the Department of History and the Department of Comparative Literature at the School of Languages, Literature, Culture and Communication, University of Limerick, Ireland. He has written and edited many books (under his own name and under a range of pseudonyms) including: *Irish Travellers: Representations and Realities* (2006) *Migrancy, Memory and Repossession: Women on the Historical Margins* (2010) and *"The Turn of the Hand": A Memoir from the Irish Margins* (with Mary Warde) (2010) an *"Insubordinate Irish": Travellers in the Text* (2011). He has written many essays and book chapters in both Irish and English and has written fiction and poetry (*Dúchas Dóchasach* (2007) in collaboration with other Irish writers including Colum McCann and Gabriel Rosenstock. Between 2006 and 2008 he was an AHRC scholar in the School of Arts, Histories and Cultures, University of Manchester. His latest book *Narratives of the Occluded Irish Diaspora* (2011) (eds. J. O'Callaghan and M. hAodha) was recently published with Peter Lang.

BIBLIOGRAPHY

Forthcoming: A short story in *Best European Fiction 2012* (Dalkey Archive Press, USA)

Where Light Begins – Haiku; Dublin: Original Writing, 2012

Uttering Her Name. Ireland: Salmon Poetry, 2009. (Poetry.)

Lacertidae; Dublin: Original Writing, 2012 (Novella) Translated from the Irish by Mícheal Ó hAodha.

My Head is Missing (Novel, Original Writing, 2012)

Tagore, Rabindranath, *Stray Birds/Éanlaith Strae*, Dublin: Salmon Poetry, 2011. (Poetic Aphorisms)

Satchidanandan, K, *Rogha Dánta*; Dublin: Original Writing, 2012 (Poetry)

Treasury of Irish Love. Poems, Proverbs & Triads, in Irish and English; New York: Hippocrene Books, 1998.

Irish Proverbs in Irish and English, Dublin: Mercier Press, 1999.

Irish Weather Wisdom. Signs of Rains, Belfast: Appletree Press, 2000.

Haiku Enlightenment, UK: Cambridge Scholars Publishing, 2009

Haiku, The Gentle Art of Disappearing UK: Cambridge Scholars Publishing, 2009